ONE DAY AT A TIME

Adult children of alcoholics can and do recover. Thousands of ACoAs are in the recovery process right now, and thousands more will be joining that process as more and more information about alcoholism and its effect on the family becomes available to the public. It must be remembered, however, that recovery is a process, not an event.

Recovery is a way of living, a quality of feeling, and a mental attitude. Every ACoA who reads this has begun the recovery process. If you had not started this process, you would not be reading this. The recovery process for ACoAs begins with the realization, or sometimes just the suspicion, that their lives are not progressing in a way that is healthy. Just the knowing that something is amiss is enough for the recovery process to start.

THE ADULT CHILDREN OF
ALCOHOLICS
SYNDROME

FROM DISCOVERY TO RECOVERY

by
Wayne Kritsberg

BANTAM BOOKS
NEW YORK · TORONTO · LONDON · SYDNEY · AUCKLAND

THE ADULT CHILDREN OF ALCOHOLICS SYNDROME
A Bantam Book / published by arrangement with Health
Communications, Inc.

PUBLISHING HISTORY
Health Communications edition published November 1985
Bantam edition / April 1988

ISBN 0-553-27279-9

Published simultaneously in the United States and Canada

Bantam Books are published by Bantam Books, a division of Random
House, Inc. Its trademark, consisting of the words "Bantam Books" and
the portrayal of a rooster, is Registered in U.S. Patent and Trademark
Office and in other countries. Marca Registrada. Bantam Books, New
York, New York.

PRINTED IN THE UNITED STATES OF AMERICA

OPM   22   21   20

Dedicated to
Marcella, my mother
Arlene, my sister

Table of Contents

Introduction   xi

PART ONE—DISCOVERY

1 The Four Major Types of Alcoholic Families   3
2 The Four Rules of the Alcoholic Family   15
3 Family Roles   25
4 The Alcoholic Family and the Healthy Family   29
5 Abandonment   32
6 Characteristics of ACoAs   39
7 Chronic Shock   49

PART TWO—RECOVERY
The Family Integration System

8 Recovery: A Process   75
9 Introduction and Setup   89
10 The Daily Log   92
11 The Family Tree   94
12 The Family Group Information Sheet   100
13 Family Myths   106
14 The Personal History Section   110
15 The Magical Child   120
16 Family Members   128
17 Influential Persons   139
18 Affirmations   141
19 Spiritual Reflections   151
20 Integration   153
21 Conclusion   156
Resources   158

Acknowledgments

There were so many people who were a part of the production of this book that it would be impossible to name them all. A special thanks must go out to the adult children of alcoholics (ACoAs) who have allowed me the privilege of being a part of their lives. For the past few years I have facilitated four ongoing therapy groups for ACoAs. It was mainly from the people in these groups that I got the written material to use as examples of work that ACoAs had done. The trust and openness of these people has transformed this book from a dream into a reality. A special thanks must also go to my friends, both personal and professional, who continued to encourage and support me during the writing of this manuscript. I would specifically like to thank Carl Kirsch, M.D., of Austin, Texas, for his assistance in preparing the section on chronic shock. Lastly, many thanks and appreciation go to Leigh McNeal, who spent many hours and late nights proofreading and helping with the rewriting of the final draft of the manuscript.

The examples used in this book are based upon actual case histories of ACoAs who are in the process of recovering from the effects of growing up in an alcoholic family. In order to insure privacy and confidentiality I have either changed the names of the persons in the example or in some cases used composites of several different people.

Introduction

The purpose of this book is twofold. First, to provide the reader with information about the adult children of alcoholics syndrome. Second, to provide a solution and a method for ACoAs to begin the recovery process. To this end the book has been divided into two primary components: Part One: Discovery and Part Two: Recovery.

Part One: Discovery focuses on the causes and consequences of the adult children of alcoholics syndrome. This section gives facts about the alcoholic family and what happens to children who are raised in this environment. It is vital that ACoAs have this information. This explains why ACoAs act and feel—or do not feel—as they do. It is very important that ACoAs understand that being raised in an alcoholic family has greatly influenced their behavior and feelings as adults. Being raised in an alcoholic family does make a difference, and this important piece of information has been overlooked for quite some time. It is also vital that therapists and other health professionals have information about ACoAs. For years, ACoAs have been misdiagnosed, misunderstood, and treated incorrectly in the professional community. This, I am happy to say, is rapidly changing.

Part Two: Recovery focuses on the recovery process. ACoAs can and do recover from the effects of being raised in an alcoholic family. Thousands are already well into recovery and leading much healthier and happier lives than they had ever dreamed possible. In this section I have presented an overview of treatment options for the ACoA and a system for recovery called the Family Integration System. The Family Integration System (FIS) is a system that I designed over a period of years that assists the ACoA in coming to terms with growing up in an alcoholic family. The system gives the ACoA a way to let go of the anger, hurt, and fear that every untreated ACoA carries buried deep inside.

ACoAs number in the millions and are recovering in the thousands. Hopefully in the near future each person who has been raised in an alcoholic family will have the necessary information and opportunity to recover from the effects of the adult children of alcoholics syndrome. It is to contribute to this end that I have written this book.

PART ONE

·

DISCOVERY

1
The Four Major Types of Alcoholic Families

People who grow up in alcoholic families have common symptoms and behaviors as a result of their common experience. It is these shared symptoms and behaviors that set adult children of alcoholics (ACoAs) apart from other people. ACoAs are different from people who were raised in other types of family systems. They view the world in a way that is unique. The common symptoms that characterize this group of people is the adult children of alcoholics syndrome.

To understand the adult children of alcoholics syndrome, it is necessary to have a knowledge of the alcoholic family. It is the alcoholic family system that causes the adult child syndrome. When children are born into this system, they are delivered into a unit that, from the beginning, inhibits their development as healthy human beings. It is of vital importance that we acknowledge, from the beginning, that the symptoms and behaviors of adult children of alcoholics are directly related to the experience of being raised in an unsafe, dysfunctional, alcoholic family system.

Some of the questions about the alcoholic family system that will be answered in the next few chapters are:

1. What is an alcoholic family system?
2. Are there different kinds of alcoholic families?
3. Are some families more alcoholic than others?
4. Are there general rules in an alcoholic family?
5. Are there general roles in the alcoholic family?

6. How does the alcoholic family compare with healthy families?

Put simply, the alcoholic family is a family in which the disease of alcoholism has affected the way the family system operates. The influence of the disease—and alcoholism is a disease—invades all aspects of family life, and the family operates in a way that is basically unhealthy. The difference between the alcoholic family system and a healthy system is that the alcoholic family system operates in a way that limits and controls the actions and emotions of the individual members. The healthy family operates to allow the individual freedom of expression and freedom to grow.

There are four major types of alcoholic family systems. The following is a description of each type of system and a diagram of that family system.

TYPE 1

This system is riddled with active alcoholism. In children, parents, grandparents, great-grandparents, and even further back in the family history, active alcoholism is rampant. Every generation of this family will have both active alcoholism and adult children of alcoholics issues to deal with.

Jane's family (see diagram below) is a typical Type 1 alcoholic family system. There is active alcoholism in every generation; her family is completely organized around drinking and those activities that can be done while drinking. When Jane came into therapy, she had been sober for almost two years, but was having a very difficult time adjusting to a sober life-style. One of her comments was "I thought all families drank like ours did. We never associated with other families or other people who were not involved in heavy drinking. Getting drunk was normal. All my uncles, aunts, and cousins drank a lot and got drunk. No one in the family thought it odd when I began to drink and get drunk at fourteen. It was sort of expected."

Not only did Jane have a whole range of ACoAs issues to deal with; she also needed to learn how live in a sober family. Jane's daughter, Mary, who was no longer living at

Type 1

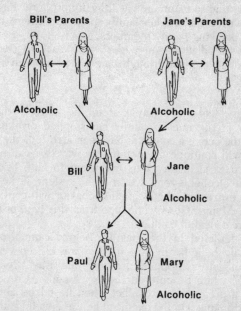

1. Bill and Jane have two children, Paul and Mary.
2. Jane's father was an alcoholic.
3. Jane is an alcoholic.
4. Of Bill and Jane's children Mary is an alcoholic.
5. Bill's father was an alcoholic.
6. Bill was not an alcoholic, but married Jane, who was an alcoholic.

home, was already recovering from alcoholism when Jane sought treatment for alcoholism. Jane's husband, Bill, was not an alcoholic, but as can be seen from the diagram he also came from an alcoholic family. Paul, age nine, was still at living at home with Jane and Bill.

For the Type 1 alcoholic family, crisis has become a life-style, a cycle which is difficult to break. In Jane's case it took concerted effort on her part, and on the part of her husband and children, to refocus the family into a nondrinking life-style. This was accomplished. Jane found, however, that to maintain a healthy atmosphere she had to limit the time she and her family spent with the rest of the actively drinking family members.

Using the diagram on page 5 it is easy to trace the disease of alcoholism through Jane's Type 1 family.

TYPE 2

In this alcoholic family system the actively drinking member of the nuclear family has stopped drinking. Although the active alcoholism has been arrested, the family system will continue to operate in a way that can only be described as alcoholic. It is important to note that even when the alcohol is removed from the system, if the family remains untreated, the alcoholic behavior will continue to operate. Many ACoAs who come from this type of system feel a great deal of conflict.

Ted, depicted in the diagram below, came from the Type 2 alcoholic family system. Ted was eleven years old when his father stopped drinking and was twenty-five years old when he entered therapy for his ACoA issues. He felt a great deal of conflict when he talked about his father's drinking. On the one hand he was grateful and happy that his father stopped drinking. On the other hand he felt angry at him. One night Ted told his group, "I feel guilty when I say that I'm angry at my father. I really am glad that he stopped drinking—and things really did get better at home when he stopped—but I still feel angry over all of those years of drinking. Not only that, but after he stopped, he never did try to spend time with me. He was always going to AA meetings or working; he never had time for me. And I'm angry at that too. I know I'm angry, but I still feel guilty, almost like I'm betraying him by talking about my anger at him."

Ted had unresolved anger at his father's behavior both before and after the drinking stopped. Like many ACoAs in Type 2 families, Ted believed he should accept, without reservation and with gratitude, his father's newfound sobriety. Ted needed treatment to learn that he had the right, the ability, and the real need to express the powerful feelings of anger, hurt, fear, and rejection he had about his father's physical abuse during the drinking days and not getting the attention he needed and deserved from his father, even in sobriety.

After Ted had been in the ACoA group awhile, he told his father that he was working on dealing with what had happened to him when he was a child. His father's comment was "Why don't you just forget what happened and go on with your life? I have." Neither Ted's mother nor his sister wanted to talk about what it was like when John, the father, was drinking. The untreated family—still acting out of fear and denial—had continued to operate alcoholically fourteen years after John, the alcoholic, had stopped drinking.

Ted's story is repeated over and over by people who come from Type 2 families. On page 8 is a diagram of Ted's Type 2 system.

TYPE 3

In the Type 3 system the active drinking has been removed from the family for one or more generations. In this system, the parents did not drink in an alcoholic way, but one of their parents—or even grandparents—was an alcoholic. Even though active drinking has not been in the family for some time, the family dynamics continue in a way that is still characteristic of an alcoholic family. Many ACoAs come from this type of family. Their parents did not abuse alcohol, but one or more of their grandparents did, and their family continues to follow the rules and behaviors of an actively drinking alcoholic family. It is extremely important for people who come from this type of system to realize that the behavioral characteristics of the disease of alcoholism are transmitted through the family, even though the active drinking has ceased.

Many times this hidden alcoholism factor will only come to light after a thorough family history has been completed. Often people from a Type 3 family will not understand why they feel so at home with ACoAs, or why they are so personally familiar with the characteristics of ACoAs.

Type 2

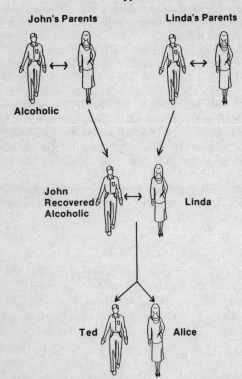

1. John and Linda have two children, Ted and Alice.
2. John's father was an alcoholic.
3. John is a recovered alcoholic.
4. Without treatment John and Linda will continue the dynamics of the alcoholic family, even though the active drinking has ceased.
5. John and Linda's children, Ted and Alice, not only are at high risk for becoming alcoholics, they will also re-create the dynamics of the alcoholic family when they have families of their own, even if they do not drink.

When they discover that alcoholism has impacted their lives from past generations, they often have a sense of relief.

Kim had a very difficult time trusting anyone: She felt full of fear. She did not even know what she was afraid of; she just felt afraid all of the time. When she got into relationships, she would become overwhelmed with fear. She would never tell her lover what she was feeling because she was afraid her lover would leave, or worse, pity her. One night a friend of Kim's took her to a ACoAs meeting. Kim felt at home for the first time in her life. But she also felt a little guilty, because neither one of her parents drank. Kim continued to go to ACoA meetings, however, because, "almost every time someone spoke in that meeting, it felt like they were telling my story. It felt like they knew exactly what I was feeling, and that they knew how I felt when I was a child."

Kim asked me if she could be in one of my ACoAs therapy groups even though her parents did not drink. When I asked her why she wanted to, she replied, "I know that my parents did not drink, but when my friends—who are all ACoAs—talk about their families, I feel like they are talking about my family. My family acted just like an alcoholic family." When Kim and I went over her family tree (see Chapter 11), it was discovered that her paternal grandfather was an alcoholic. I explained to Kim about the alcoholic family rules (see Chapter 2), and that even though her father did not drink, he was raised in an alcoholic family and learned their rules. Kim's father had used the same system in raising his own children. No wonder Kim felt so at home at ACoAs meetings; she followed the same alcoholic family rules as her friends. Although she didn't know it, Kim came from an alcoholic family. She was only one generation removed from the active drinking.

Kim's story is not unusual. Many ACoAs come from an alcoholic family in which the active drinking has skipped one, or sometimes more, generations. The diagram on page 10 shows Kim's Type 3 alcoholic family.

TYPE 4

In this nonalcoholic family one of its members becomes an alcoholic. The family then becomes an alcoholic family

Type 3

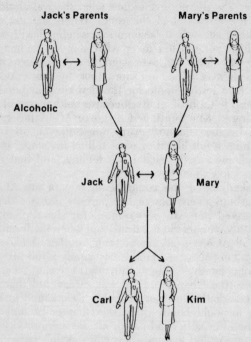

1. Jack and Mary have two children, Carl and Kim.
2. Jack's father was an alcoholic.
3. Neither Jack nor Mary drink, but because Jack's father was an alcoholic, the dynamics of an alcoholic family will be continued in Jack and Mary's family.
4. Jack will clearly have ACoA issues to resolve.
5. Jack and Mary's children will have ACoA issues, and if untreated, will create families of their own that have the characteristics of the alcoholic family system.
6. Both of Jack and Mary's children will also be at high risk for active alcoholism.

system. The children of this family will have ACoAs issues and will be at high risk for becoming alcoholic themselves. As the disease of alcoholism progresses in the alcoholic member, the family becomes more and more dysfunctional in its attempts to deal with the alcoholic's behavior.

There are many kinds of nonalcoholic dysfunctional families. First-generation alcoholics often come from dysfunctional families.

When I first saw Carol as a client, she had been sober for two years. No one in her family ever drank. She had checked her family history as far back as her great-grandparents on both sides, and nowhere was there even a hint of alcoholism. It was clear, however, that Carol's drinking had been out of control. Although she did not drink on a daily basis, when she did drink, she lost control, got drunk, had blackouts, and did things that she normally would not do. She could not predict her behavior when she drank. She also hid her supply of alcohol—in her case, wine—and hid her empty bottles. When she finally cleaned out her garage and saw how many empty wine bottles there were, Carol became convinced of her alcoholism.

Even though there was no alcoholism present, Carol's family was dysfunctional. There was never any real communication of feelings in her family. As she put it, "I grew up in an emotional vacuum. My family never showed emotion to one another, especially love or affection. I never remember my dad hugging me as a kid." Carol also reported that there were often angry and sometimes violent outbursts by her father, and she lived in fear of these incidents. Her family clearly did not demonstrate good health. Carol's two children, who were teenagers when she got sober, definitely came from a first-generation alcoholic family and would have ACoAs issues to deal with. The diagram on page 12 shows Carol's Type 4 alcoholic family.

When looking at the four major types of alcoholic families, it is important to consider two things: First, the effects of alcoholism on the family occur even when the active drinking is not present. Second, the alcoholic system will re-create itself generation after generation if the family is not treated. These points are important. A great number of ACoAs come from families where there is no alcoholic drinking taking place. If alcoholism is in their family history, they will have ACoA issues.

Type 4

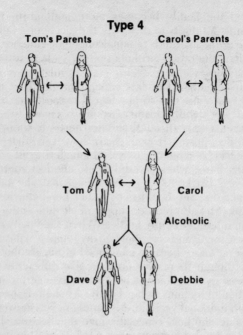

1. Carol and Tom have two children, Debbie and Dave.
2. Carol's family has no alcoholism.
3. Carol is an alcoholic.
4. Tom has no history of alcoholism in his family, and is not an alcoholic.
5. Carol and Tom's children, Debbie and Dave, will have ACoA issues, and be at high risk for alcoholism.

Although there are four general types of alcoholic family systems, there is no typical alcoholic family. Each family is unique. Within the four general types of alcoholic families there is a wide variation of family dysfunction. It is safe to state that every alcoholic family is an unhealthy family, but there are degrees of dysfunction within different families. The degree of family dysfunction has a direct effect on the amount of emotional and physical damage that is done to the children. The more dysfunctional the family, the greater the damage to the child.

At one extreme of the continuum of functional/dysfunctional family systems is the extremely violent system, in which physical violence occurs on a regular basis among the family members. In this system the death of a child from physical abuse can—and sometimes does—occur. Children surviving this system often have severe emotional trauma that deeply affects their adult lives. It is important to remember that in the violent system it is not only the alcoholic who commits acts of violence in the family; the other adults in the family are often violent to each other and to the children. Siblings often physically take out their anger and frustration on weaker and younger brothers and sisters. Sibling abuse can be as terrifying and as damaging to a child as parental physical abuse.

At the same end of the continuum of functional/dysfunctional family systems can be the family in which there is no physical violence, or even any shouting or displays of anger. This family may look like a family that is functioning at a healthy level, but within the family the alcoholic behaviors of the members create a system that is extremely stressful on its members. Children in this system often live in quiet terror and abandonment. No one in the family actually physically hurts them, but the threat of harm is a constant presence. Emotional damage to the children in a nonphysically violent system can be as harmful to these children as physical violence is for the children living in a violent system.

Also, at the same end of the functional/dysfunctional continuum is the sexually abusing alcoholic family. Sexual abuse is as damaging to the child as in either of the above situations. It is important to recognize that sexual abuse is common in alcoholic families. Sexual abuse can range from continuing sexual intercourse over a long period of time to single sexual incidents, such as fondling. It must also be recognized that sexual abuse includes nonphysical abuse; inappropriate sexual comments and sexual teasing on the part of the adult often have a traumatic emotional impact on both male and female children.

The following is the Family System Continuum Chart. The continuum ranges from –10 to +10. The severely dysfunctional families are grouped at the −10 end of the scale, and the highly functional families are grouped at the + 10 end of the scale.

The Family System Continuum Chart

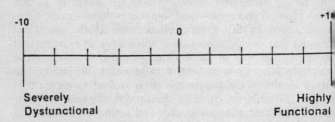

Looking at the above continuum, we can state several things about alcoholic families:

1. The alcoholic family will always fall between 0 and −10 on this continuum because it is always a dysfunctional family. It differs from other alcoholic families only in degree of dysfunction.

2. There is always emotional abuse in alcoholic families. Physical and sexual abuse are common in these families, and each can be equally damaging to the child. Depending on the severity of the abuse, the family rating will be toward the lower end (−10) of the continuum.

3. The more severe the family dysfunction, the greater the emotional damage to the children. Many alcoholic families combine emotional, physical, and sexual abuse. The Family System Continuum will be used again to compare, in more detail, healthy and unhealthy families.

2
The Four Rules of the Alcoholic Family

Originally the family system established rules of behavior and roles for its members so the family could adjust to having an active alcoholic as a member. The rules and roles that were imposed on the individual members of the family were survival techniques, and although the family survived, the patterns of behavior that were established in the family were unhealthy.

It is important to understand that the rules and roles of the alcoholic family did not just happen; they were a response to, and a way to deal with, having an active alcoholic as a part of the family. The rules and roles are an attempt to bring order and stability to an increasingly chaotic and unstable situation.

There are four general rules that operate in the alcoholic family. These rules are:

1. the Rule of Rigidity
2. the Rule of Silence
3. the Rule of Denial
4. the Rule of Isolation

Viewing the chart below, it can be seen that at the core of every alcoholic family is the disease of alcoholism. Even though active drinking may no longer be in the system, the rules will continue to operate and will be passed from one generation to another.

The Alcoholic Family System

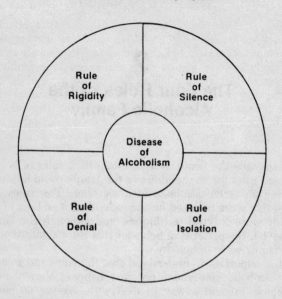

To one degree or another the above rules apply to all alcoholic families. When children grow up in alcoholic families, these rules, which are learned, become a part of the way they as adults respond to the world. They become an unconscious code of conduct. Because these rules are so ingrained into the children of the alcoholic family, when these children grow up, they have a tendency to search out people who follow the same rules. They feel comfortable with people who know the rules. That's why so many adult children of alcoholics become involved with either active alcoholics (or other drug users), or with people who also come from alcoholic families. Time and time again I've heard ACoAs say, "I don't understand why, over and over again, I seem to get into relationships with the same kind of people." This happens because they seek people who have the same code of conduct, even though their rational mind may tell them that this relationship will be yet another painful disaster.

THE RULE OF RIGIDITY

The alcoholic family is inflexible. It cannot adapt to change easily, nor does it willingly allow family members to change. This rigid behavior manifests itself in all aspects of family life and has its roots in the way the family attempts to deal with having an alcoholic as a member. One of the effects of alcoholism on an individual is unpredictable behavior. As the alcoholism progresses, the behavior of the alcoholic becomes increasingly unpredictable, and the family continually adjusts to this unpredictable behavior. In order to bring some stability to the family, more and more rigid rules of behavior are imposed on the nonalcoholic members of the family. As the family adapts to the alcoholic's increasingly unpredictable behavior, it becomes increasingly rigid.

The rigidity of the alcoholic family system is easily observed in the way the family influences its children. In order for children to grow, mature, and to develop healthy social interactions, they need a place where there is room for them to experiment with life. They need a safe place where they can try different ways of behaving, and where they can change and grow. The alcoholic family does not provide the kind of flexible environment that children need in order to experiment with life.

The alcoholic family, in fact, provides just the opposite. Because of its rigid structure, the children in the system are not allowed to grow emotionally. The parents try to keep the children children. This does not mean that children get no responsibility—they very often do. They get the responsibility to take care of parents, brothers, sisters, and to do household duties, but they never get the opportunity to develop emotionally into adults. The system is rigid and fixes the children as children. When these children become adults, they are in most cases still children emotionally. This is particularly obvious when ACoAs are relating to their parents. They almost always have "little kid" feelings when they are interacting with their parents.

Manny, a thirty-five-year-old ACoA, summed up this feeling when he said, "I'm a grown man, and when I am with my parents, I feel like I am five years old. I am afraid to speak up for myself, and I walk around like I'm on pins and needles."

Paradoxically, although Manny responded like a child emotionally when he was with his parents, he felt that he did not have a childhood. He often stated that he "always felt like an adult." He, like many ACoAs, felt that he had lost his childhood—that he had never really been able to experience the freedom and joy of being a child.

Growing up with the rule of rigidity translates, as an adult, into a need to control. The ACoA need to control is directly related to childhood experiences. ACoAs learned that rigid rules of behavior are the way to control unpredictable situations. This often translates into: Life and people are unpredictable; therefore, there is a need to control all aspects of life, including other people. This control means no spontaneity, and without spontaneity, there can be no playfulness or any real happiness. ACoAs are generally very serious people.

THE RULE OF SILENCE

Members of alcoholic families are bound by a rule of silence: They cannot talk about what is happening in the family. This rule of silence extends not only to talking to people outside of the family, but also includes talking to the members of the family itself. The rule of silence not only bans talking about the behavior and actions of the family, it also bans talking about feelings. This no-talk rule is so strong that children who grow up in this family system have difficulty in expressing themselves for the rest of their lives. The rule of nonexpression follows them, and they in turn teach it to their children.

In examining this rule of silence, it is important to remember that the alcoholic family system has a vested interest in keeping its members quiet about what goes on inside of the system. Keeping silent is not just expedient but necessary for the system to function. If there were open and free communication in the system, individual members of the system would be forced to change. Change is the last thing that the alcoholic system is equipped to handle, i.e., the Rule of Rigidity.

Children growing up in this silent system learn at a very early age that it is not okay to talk about certain things. Any discussion on the child's part about drinking, behavior that is related to drinking, or other nonsocially accepted behaviors such as physical abuse or incest, is quickly squelched. The child is unable to talk about what he or she sees or hears. This inability to talk about what is seen or heard has a direct effect on how the child will relate to the world. Without being able to do any reality checking, the child is forced to interpret the events in his or her life without the input from caring adults. As adults, these children often have difficulty asking questions. They feel that they should know the answers. And, of course, they don't, so they guess.

This silence extends not to just what the child sees, but also to what the child feels. Along with not having permission to talk about what is seen, the child is not permitted to talk about any feelings that he or she may have as a result of alcoholic behavior.

The fear, anger, and hurt—core issues for adult children of alcoholics—have their roots in the inability of the family system to cope with these powerful feelings. As children experience the terror, rage, and grief that are directly related to the alcoholic behavior of the family, they cope by attempting to repress their feelings. They cannot talk to anyone about how they feel, so they cope the best way they can. The child living in an alcoholic family is like a pressure cooker on a stove. As the temperature goes up, the pressure inside the cooker increases. Instead of bleeding the pressure off slowly, by talking, the child responds by adding thicker walls. Occasionally the pressure gets too high, and the child acts out and blows off some steam, but most of the pressure is kept inside and remains there for the rest of his or her life, unless he or she gets treatment.

Mary, an ACoA, had a father who liked to drink and drive. When he would go to bars and get drunk, he would often take Mary with him. Although Mary liked being with her father, she would be terrified when he was drunk and driving. Often her father would have accidents, and drive the car into ditches or hit poles and trees. None of the accidents were major, but still Mary became terrified whenever her father would drive. At eleven years of age Mary learned to drive by pushing her father out from behind the wheel of the car, after he had passed out, and then driving the car home herself. She did this for a number of years.

Until Mary entered treatment, she had never told anyone about the fear that she had of driving with her father, and she had never told anyone about having to drive her father home. One of the results of Mary's having to keep her fear to herself, and never talking about having to drive her father home was that she became extremely frightened when she was not driving. As an adult Mary felt that she had to drive or something terrible would happen. After processing her fear and talking about her feelings of having to drive her father home when he was drunk, Mary lost some of this fear. Today, although Mary still prefers to drive, she will let another person drive.

The only way ACoAs can get free of the rule of silence is by talking about what happened to them and expressing their repressed feelings. Mary's case was not an extreme. All ACoAs have the rule of silence, which operates at the expense of both the ACoA's emotional well-being and ability to function honestly and openly in the world.

THE RULE OF DENIAL

The denial of the alcoholic family begins with the denial that there is any problem with alcohol. As the behavior of the family members become more and more dysfunctional, the denial becomes stronger and stronger. Denial is one of the cornerstones of the system. If the system can continue to deny what is happening, then it will not have to change.

The people, particularly the children, of this system are surrounded by denial on all sides. What they see with their eyes, hear with their ears, and feel in their hearts they are told is not true. Not only are they told to ignore the behavior of the alcoholic, but they are also told to pretend that nothing is wrong—to pretend to be normal.

It is important to realize that when I use the word *told*, I do not necessarily mean the spoken word. Although the alcoholic family rarely communicates directly with words, it does communicate to its members in a variety of other ways. Nondirective talking, body language, and the "look" from parents that most ACoAs are familiar with are some of the ways the alcoholic family communicates.

The conflict between what the child sees happening in the family and what the child is told to believe is happening is one of the basic conflicts of ACoAs. They are continually trying to figure out what is going on and separate what is real from what is not real. They learn not to trust—either themselves or others. The children in the alcoholic family hear the family say, "We are a happy family and we stick together, and they see the adults in the family fighting and belittling each other. They see Mom passed out drunk every day when they come home from school and are told, "Everything is fine, and don't tell anyone about Mom being sick." The denial of reality is a fundamental issue for ACoAs.

This denial also extends to feelings. When painful events occur, the feelings that naturally accompany those events are denied, because people are not "supposed" to have these feelings. Sara, an ACoA, told her AcoAs group, "I do not feel anger, I have never felt anger, and I do not think I will ever feel anger." Anger, Sara learned from her mother, was not a nice emotion, and good girls did not express anger. Of course, what she saw at home was a lot of angry people, sometimes shouting at each other and sometimes even hitting each other. There was no room in the family for her anger. It was downright dangerous for her to be angry. The result was her denial of her own anger, and the ability to ever express anger or to deal with people who expressed anger.

The reality was that Sara was one of the angriest people in the ACoAs group. When she finally allowed some of her repressed anger/rage to be expressed, she reported an intense feeling of freedom and a sense of dropping a heavy load.

Children model the behaviors of the adults in their lives. This is one of the ways they learn to become healthy human beings. In the alcoholic family the denial of feelings is so prevalent that children never learn how to honestly express emotions. They see the adults in the family walk around smiling on the outside and boiling with rage on the inside; the inside emotions and the outside expressions on the family members rarely match. When the children of this family grow up, they will smile when they are angry, look blank when they are hurt, and remain in constant conflict with how they feel on the inside and what they show on the outside.

If I pretend that this is not happening, then maybe it will go away is the motto by which many ACoAs live their lives. Denying reality—particularly painful reality—is second nature. The it-will-be-different-this-time way of looking (or not looking) at the world gets the ACoA into many painful situations, particularly in sexual relationships. Many ACoAs will stay with a partner, pretending time after time that things are going to be different, and, of course, they never are. They get worse.

THE RULE OF ISOLATION

The alcoholic family is a closed system. It resists the movement of its members in and out of the system and resists adding outsiders as members. The members cling emotionally to each other, but never become intimate. The alcoholic system tries to be self-sufficient. It creates the myth that no one outside the system will understand and that no one outside of the system is to be trusted.

The system cannot afford to have people outside of the family know what is happening in the system. Therefore some alcoholic families have a tendency to move from place to place. The family moves because it cannot bear the scrutiny of its neighbors. As the alcoholic behaviors become more and more extreme, the family becomes more and more isolated.

The family that does not move a lot is often as isolated from its neighbors as the family that does move. I have often heard clients like Harry, who lived in a small town while he was growing up, say, "I lived next door to people for years and never spoke to them."

At first glance it would seem that the isolation of the alcoholic family would serve to draw the family together.

Although many alcoholic families have the them-against-us attitude, the individual members are as isolated from each other as the family is isolated from the community. This is an important point, so I'll repeat it: The alcoholic family isolates itself from the community, and the individual members of the family isolate themselves from each other.

The alcoholic family myth of "We will be there for you when you need us" is just not true. The alcoholic family is incapable of supporting its members emotionally or spiritually. They cannot be there during a crisis or at any other time. The individual members are isolated from each other, and when the children grow up, they continue to isolate from other people. Their feelings of loneliness run very deep.

Michael, a thirty-two-year-old ACoA, continually complained of being lonely, even when he was in a relationship. He really wanted to have intimacy, but he did not know how. He felt, like many ACoAs, that he was missing something that other people seemed to have. One of his statements was "I used to think that sex meant intimacy. Now I know that it is more than that, but what, I'm not sure." Growing up in an alcoholic family, Michael never had a chance to find out what intimacy was.

The very nature of the alcoholic family inhibits the development of intimate relationships. Michael's family had a very rigid structure. The family did not talk about what was going on, feelings and facts about behavior were denied, and he learned to isolate from other people in order to protect himself and survive. Michael had never had a chance when it came to developing intimate relationships. His whole way of viewing the world was opposed to the development of intimacy. Michael was a very typical ACoA.

Every ACoA is co-dependent; it cannot be helped. The adult child was raised to follow a set of four rules that insure the development of co-dependency. I define co-dependency as the condition of a person who is emotionally dependent on an outside source to get feelings of self-esteem and who focuses on external stimuli in order not to feel his or her own pain. All ACoAs fall within this broad definition of co-dependence. As the ACoA works to resolve the painful issues of growing up in an alcoholic family, the co-dependency is also treated. It is important to state that while it is true that all ACoAs are co-dependent, not all co-dependent people are ACoAs. Many co-dependents are raised in nonalcoholic dysfunctional family systems or learn co-dependent behavior when they become involved in unhealthy relationships.

The ACoA is bound by the four rules of the alcoholic family. They use these rules as a way to live their lives. They really have little choice in the matter; this is how they learned to live and to survive as children. To become healthy and begin to live full and happy lives ACoAs must begin to break the rules of the alcoholic family. This is neither an easy nor a quick process, but it is being done by thousands of ACoAs who are not content to remain bound by chains of rigidity, silence, denial, and isolation.

3
Family Roles

In order to survive the rules of the alcoholic family system, the individual members of the system often adapt by taking on various roles. These roles are a natural extension of the family rules. When the members of the family have fixed roles, their behavior is predictable. The roles reduce the possibility of spontaneous behavior on the part of the family members. The alcoholic family is a very chaotic system, and the roles provide some stability. They also divert attention from the often bizarre behavior of the family to the behavior of the member who is playing a role.

Each role serves the purpose of trying to maintain the status quo, and each person cast in a particular role is playing that role in order to survive a fearful and dangerous situation. The creation of roles is a direct result of the family members trying to cope with the disease of alcoholism. As the disease progresses, the rules and roles become more and more fixed and rigid.

Using a fixed model of family roles is an effective tool to teach and to understand the dynamics of the alcoholic family. In reality, however, the family is much too complex to be put into a model. The roles that are most associated with the alcoholic family are often blended in actual family situations. Also, over a period of time, individual family members may play various roles according to the needs of the family. Below are some of the more common roles:

1. The Hero: Tries to make the family look good by achieving success in school or work.
2. The Scapegoat: Diverts attention from the family by getting into trouble.
3. The Lost One: Hides out, tries not to make waves, draws attention by nonpresence.
4. The Clown: Lessens tension in the family by being funny and cute.
5. The Placater: Tries to reduce conflict in the family by smoothing things over.
6. The Enabler: Prevents the alcoholic from experiencing the consequences of his or her alcoholic behavior.

The above roles are only generalizations of the roles that appear in alcoholic families. In the family, roles often become blended. It is not uncommon to have a Clown-Placater type, or a Hero-Scapegoat type. The combinations that evolve in the alcoholic family are astounding. Although the above roles are the most common and well-known, the alcoholic family is not limited to using just those; roles will be created based on the needs of the family.

One of the characteristics of the alcoholic family is having fixed roles for its members. Peter is an example of a ACoA who maintained a fixed role throughout his life. He was the Hero. He was an extremely successful stockbroker and had many material assets, including a large bank account. He was not an alcoholic. All of his life, as far back as he could remember, he had been successful. He had been at the top of his class at school, excelled in sports, seemed to have boundless energy, and engaged successfully in many activities. Peter's father, who was an alcoholic, failed at everything he tried to do. Peter assumed the role of Hero and tried to bring success to the family.

At age thirty-five, when he entered therapy, Peter was at the peak of his career. In spite of all of his material successes, his marriage—to an active alcoholic—was falling apart. He felt that no matter what he did, it was never enough. He felt worthless and viewed himself as a failure. Peter was typical of many Hero types. His external world looked great, as though he had everything anyone could want. His internal life, however, was full of self-doubt, feelings of worthlessness, and fear of failing.

There are a significant number of instances where family members who are in fixed roles evolve into other roles or combinations of roles. The Scapegoat can become the Hero; the Lost One can become the Scapegoat. Although these changes generally occur over a period of time, sudden changes in the family, such as death, divorce, or blending with another alcoholic family (after a divorce and a remarriage with another alcoholic or ACoAs), can cause abrupt changes in the family roles.

When Betty, an ACoA, was a small child, she was primarily in the role of the Lost One. She would stay in her room and read or play with her stereo. She never really got in anyone's way, and her school activities did not stand out. Compared to the rest of the family, she was almost invisible. When she became an adolescent, she began to get into trouble at school, and started to make waves at home. The Scapegoat-type behavior continued through high school and into college. After college Betty became a Hero and quite successful.

Betty also became an alcoholic and received treatment for her alcoholism when she was twenty-eight. After she had been sober for two years, she joined an ACoAs group. During group she said she felt confused about her changing roles. She felt that she had moved from being a Lost One, to a Scapegoat, to being a Hero, and now she felt she retained characteristics of all three roles.

Betty's story is not unusual. Many ACoAs move through different roles as they grow older. One ACoAs, an only child, reported that at various times during his childhood and teenage years, he felt that he played all of the above roles.

In one way or another all of the roles that are played in the alcoholic family enable the alcoholic to continue to drink and act in a way that is both self-destructive and harmful to the other members of the family. Family members enable the alcoholic to continue on the path of self-destruction by adapting to the alcoholic's behavior rather then confronting it. An ACoA named Rick summed up his enabling behavior when he said, "I never thought of myself as an enabler of my father's drinking. I now see that my silence about what I saw and felt about his drinking really enabled him to continue to drink. Even though I was an adult, I still enabled him with my denial and silence."

The importance of using roles as a method of identifying behavioral characteristics is unquestioned. It must be remembered, however, that the roles are a response to the rules of the alcoholic family, and the rules of the family are a response to the disease of alcoholism. The adult child must look beneath the rules and the roles and find the emotional states that exist. It is the releasing of the emotional states—with the underlying fear, anger, and hurt—that is one of the major cornerstones of recovery for ACoAs.

4
The Alcoholic Family and the Healthy Family

The alcoholic family and the healthy family are at opposite ends of the spectrum. The alcoholic family operates in a way that contains and controls the members of the system. This control stifles the mental, emotional, and sometimes physical growth of its members. The healthy family, on the other hand, assists its members in their development. The controls that the healthy family places on its members are appropriate to the age group and the abilities of the individual members.

Once again let's look at the Family System Continuum. As before, the chart is scaled from –10 to +10, with –10 being the low end or most dysfunctional end, and +10 being the high or most functional end. The alcoholic family will always fall in the 0 to –10 range, depending on the degree of dysfunction; by its nature the alcoholic family is dysfunctional. Listed below the 0 to –10 side of the Family System Continuum are ten characteristics of the alcoholic family. Below the 0 to +10 side of the continuum are listed ten corresponding characteristics of the healthy family.

There are several points that can be made about the continuum on page 30. First, I have never met a totally unhealthy (–10) family, nor have I ever met a totally healthy (+10) family. Second, most alcoholic families that I have encountered would fall in the –2 to –6 range, depending on the inflexibility of the family. The same is true for the healthy family. Most would fall in the 0 to +5 range, depending on family flexibility. Third, the healthy family

The Family System Continuum

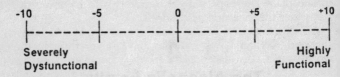

-10   -5   0   +5   +10

Severely   Highly
Dysfunctional   Functional

Alcoholic Family	Healthy Family
1. Rigid rules.	1. No rigid rules.
2. Rigid roles.	2. No rigid roles.
3. Family secrets.	3. No family secrets.
4. Resists outsiders entering the system.	4. Allows outsiders into the system.
5. Is very serious.	5. Has a sense of humor.
6. No personal privacy; unclear personal boundaries.	6. Members have right to personal privacy and develop a sense of self.
7. False loyalty to the family; members are never free to leave the system.	7. Members have a sense of family and are permitted to leave the system.
8. Conflict between members is denied and ignored.	8. Conflict between members is allowed and resolved.
9. The family resists change.	9. The family continually changes.
10. There is no unity; the family is fragmented.	10. There is a sense of wholeness.

can, for a short period of time, act in a very dysfunctional way, depending on the nature of the family crisis. The healthy family, however, does not remain in a dysfunctional mode of operation for an extended period of time. It will reassert its health and return to a normal state. This is not true for the alcoholic family. Crisis increases the amount and intensity of dysfunction, and the family does not recover. It gets worse.

From the above Family System Continuum and the following descriptions of the alcoholic family and the healthy family, it can be seen that the person who grows up in an alcoholic family will view life in a different way from the person who comes from a healthy one. The ACoA's basic approach to life is different. ACoAs view the world as an unsafe place and cope with an unsafe world by using the rules that they learned as children.

An ACoA named Millie spoke for many ACoAs when she said, "When I was growing up, I never thought the world was a safe place. Even today, whenever I put my foot down, I wonder if the earth will really be there."

5
Abandonment

Every person who is raised in an alcoholic family experiences abandonment. The alcoholic family, because of its preoccupation with alcoholism, cannot fully nurture a child. Neither parent, either alcoholic or co-dependent, is able to supply the child with consistent love and support. There are two major types of abandonment that the ACoA experiences: physical and emotional.

Physical Abandonment

Physical abandonment is when a child is left alone by his parents and its basic physical needs are not met. Physical abandoment of small children can come in many forms. The most common are:

1. Missed feedings or meals.
2. Long periods of time with unchanged and soiled diapers.
3. Children left alone for hours and sometime days.
4. Infants left in the care of older brothers or sisters who are still children themselves.

The misconception that abandonment is when the parents "give the child up," or "leave the child on the church steps," is just that—a misconception. Most children born into alcoholic families are raised in that environment. Many of these children suffer from repeated physical abandonments. All too often what is publicized are the cases in which the child or children are left alone to fend for themselves for days. Although this does occur—sometimes with tragic results—most of the physical abandonment that ACoAs experience is of shorter duration, generally hours rather than days.

The repeated physical abandonment leaves the child with a core of fear and loneliness that extends into adulthood. The reinforced message that "you are in the way and not wanted" is a message that ACoAs receive as children and keep with them.

Emotional Abandonment

The emotional abandonment that a child in an alcoholic family experiences is often as devastating to the child as physical abandonment. ACoAs often state that they cannot understand why they feel so abandoned; they know that their parents never left them alone, and that all of their physical needs were met. What these ACoAs are suffering from is emotional abandonment, which, to one degree or another, all ACoAs experience.

Emotional abandonment occurs when the parent, although there physically, is not there emotionally. The parent's focus on either drinking, the person who is drinking, or (as in the Type 3 Alcoholic Family) the behavior of the family. Regardless of where the focus is, it is not on the child. Although the physical needs of the child are met, there is no nurturing, hugging, or emotional intimacy developed. Children know when a parent is not there for them emotionally; this emotional abandonment can, and does, have far-reaching effects on the ACoA. The deep sense of worthlessness that ACoAs experience is directly related to being abandoned as children. The more severe the abandonment, the deeper the sense of worthlessness.

Children are not born into the world as blank pieces of paper. They have a whole set of emotions, and at a very early age can perceive the emotions of their parents. Current research indicates that even before birth the unborn child has emotions and reacts to the emotional state of both the mother and, to a lesser degree, the father.

ACoAs who have been emotionally abandoned have good reason to fear abandonment as adults. They have been abandoned, time and time again, as children. The message that they got from their parents was the same as those ACoAs who were physically abandoned: You are in the way and not wanted.

Abandonment sparks fear in the child. If we try to view the world as a child, we can get a sense of what this fear is like. A child cannot take care of him- or herself. Without adults—parents, in most cases—children would not survive. This is not a theory. A two-year-old child left to its own devices would die. Kids are not capable of taking care of themselves, and they know it. Children may not be able to verbalize the fear of their parents' leaving and not coming back, but that fear is there. A child, when abandoned, experiences a fear that is primal. It is the fear of not surviving—the fear of dying.

The following chart is an emotional matrix of a typical ACoA.

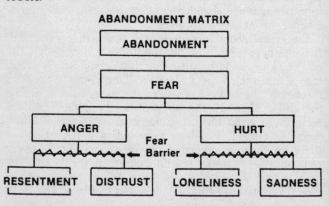

ABANDONMENT MATRIX

ABANDONMENT

FEER → FEAR

ANGER   HURT

Fear Barrier

RESENTMENT   DISTRUST   LONELINESS   SADNESS

Let's look more closely at this chart, reading from the top down.

Abandonment

This is a core issue for ACoAs. Many ACoAs, because of the nature of the alcoholic family, experience physical abandonment; all experience emotional abandonment. Many often experience a combination of both.

Fear

The fear that ACoAs always have, at the core of their being, is the primal one of not being certain they will survive. Although most ACoAs cannot identify where this fear comes from, they often will state that they have unnamed fears, and they are always afraid. Because the fear was established in the ACoA at a very early age, its roots are unknown to the ACoA, and ACoAs are generally baffled as to why they are so afraid. The feeling of fear is so overwhelming to the ACoA that its energy is diverted into hurt and anger.

Anger

The overwhelming sense of fear that the ACoA has as a result of abandonment will be expressed in the feeling of anger. The anger is a way to deal with the fear. Anger is manifested in resentment and distrust. The resentment at the parents by ACoAs, which is easy to understand, is a direct result of the children not understanding why this is happening to them. Their "knowers" know that they deserve better than this. The resentment is, in reality, anger and rage that is controlled, repressed, and transformed into resentment because the alcoholic family is not generally a safe place to show anger.

The distrust that ACoAs have of the world is directly related to not being able to trust their parents. Their parents were not there for them when they needed them. Therefore ACoAs developed deep, general distrust of the world and the people in it. It is important to note that a child's primary view of the world is developed through the relationship the child has with his or her parents.

Hurt

The overwhelming fear that the ACoA experiences as a result of abandonment manifests in the feeling of deep

hurt, which includes the feelings of loneliness and sadness. Many ACoAs have such a deep well of loneliness
that no matter how many friends they have or relationships
they develop, the feeling never leaves them. This loneliness is a direct result of being abandoned as a child. There
is also a sorrow that runs deep in ACoAs—so deep that
many ACoAs are unaware that this sadness exists inside
them. The sorrow and sadness are a direct result of the
knowing that their parents abandoned them, knowing that
they were left alone by the people who were most important in their lives.

There is an equal amount of hurt and anger in the
ACoAs. Many ACoAs have developed the ability to mani-
fest one or the other of these two emotions. As a rule—and
this is a *very* general rule—men have an easier time
displaying anger and women have an easier time displaying hurt. Most ACoAs are one-sided in their ability to
display emotions. It is important to know that even though
ACoAs can display anger, they also have tears and hurt that
are present and repressed. An ACoAs who can show tears
also represses an equal amount of rage.

Looking again the Abandonment Matrix on page 34, we
can see that there is a barrier of fear between the hurt and
anger, and the outer emotions of resentment, distrust,
sadness, and loneliness. This barrier of fear prevents the
ACoA from both acknowledging and feeling the core issues of fear, hurt, and anger. The fear is present because
of the overwhelming power that the ACoA senses in these
emotions. Many ACoAs make statements like "If I begin
to cry, I don't think I will ever stop," or "If I ever let my
anger out, I will lose control and kill someone." These
fears are very real to the ACoA and are not to be dis-
counted. The ACoA feels that he or she must maintain
tight control over feelings. This compulsion to control
spills over into all other aspects of life.

Sid, a forty-year-old ACoA, said, "I don't do tears.
Sometimes I get a feeling of hurt. It will seem to come up
from deep down inside of me. It's almost like a physical
pain in my chest and behind my eyes. I'll feel like I want
to cry, but nothing will come, and I really don't want to
cry—I'm afraid to. I'm afraid that if I ever start to cry, I'll

never stop." Sid's experience is duplicated again and again by ACoAs. Not only for hurt, but also for anger. Carmen, a thirty-two-year-old AcoA, said almost the same thing when she told her ACoAs group that she never got angry. Her statement was, "I never get angry. I'm afraid to. I'm afraid if I ever got angry, I would lose control, and I would be locked up, and the key thrown away." These are very common thoughts for most ACoAs to have.

The emotions of resentment, distrust, sadness, and loneliness on the emotional matrix are those emotions that are most accessible to the ACoA. These emotional states, although not talked about by most ACoAs, are acknowledged by many ACoAs to be present in their lives. The resentment, distrust, sadness, and loneliness are feeling states the ACoA has learned to live with, although this is not the picture that he or she tries to present to the world. The ACoA tries to hide feelings and pretend to be just like everyone else. These behavioral fronts will be discussed more fully in Chapter 6.

The Abandonment/Engulfment Phenomenon

All ACoAs have issues around abandonment, and some ACoAs also have issues around abandonment/engulfment. Engulfment is when the parent feels guilty for abandoning and neglecting the child, and tries to make up for this by smothering the child with attention.

The "I love you—go away" message was very firmly programmed into an ACoA named Jake. As a boy he lived with his mother—an alcoholic—and his younger sister. His mother, who was the only adult in his life, would go on drinking binges and disappear for three or four days at a time. Jake, at age eight, was responsible for taking care of his sister. He would borrow money from neighbors for food for the two of them. Sometimes he would even steal food. When Jake's mother would get sober enough to realize she needed to go home and take care of her family, she would arrive with gifts and lavish affection on both Jake and his sister, telling them both that she was sorry and would never leave again. But Jake's mother repeated this pattern until her death. By that time Jake was a teenager living away from home.

Jake reported having lots of difficulty in sexual relationships. When he was attracted to someone, he would smother the person with affection, then would become very afraid and withdraw emotionally from the relationship. He would repeat this pattern until his partner would become fed up and leave—or until he himself could not stand it any longer and would break up the relationship.

Jake's was a classic case of abandonment/engulfment. During group therapy Jake would demonstrate the same affection/withdrawal behavior with the group that occurred in his relationships. Over a period of time he was able, little by little, to break the pattern of behavior that he learned as a child from his mother. It was difficult work for him, but he persevered and learned that he could stop smothering people with affection and they would still like him. He also learned to trust that most people were not like his mother, and that he did not have to continue to retreat into withdrawal and isolation to protect himself.

The abandonment/engulfment phenomenon is fairly common in ACoAs. When the parent abandons the child, either physically, emotionally, or both, the parent, feeling guilty, often smothers the child with affection and love. Of course, this smothering of the child is only for a short period of time, until the next abandonment. This inconsistent behavior constantly keeps the child off-balance. The ACoA learns at a very early age the "I love you—go away" message.

As adults, many ACoAs are baffled by the way they treat those they love. They act the way they have been taught by their parents: "I love you—go away." The ACoA strongly desires intimacy and tries to achieve it by smothering the person with whom he or she wishes to be intimate, and then the ACoA pushes that person away.

6

Characteristics of ACoAs

A person who is raised in an alcoholic family, because of the four family rules of Rigidity, Silence, Denial, and Isolation, develops a set of characteristics that are similar to others who are raised in the same kind of system. These similar characteristics shared by ACoAs can be grouped into four main categories:

1. emotional characteristics
2. mental characteristics
3. physical characteristics
4. behavioral characteristics

ACoAs Characteristics Grouping Chart

Emotional Characteristics	Mental Characteristics	Physical Characteristics	Behavioral Characteristics
Fear	Thinking in absolutes	Tense shoulders	Crisis-oriented living
Anger	Lack of information	Lower back pain	Manipulative behavior
Hurt	Compulsive thinking	Sexual dysfunction	Intimacy problems
Resentment	Indecision	Gastro-intestinal disorders	Unable to have fun
Distrust	Learning disabilities	Stress-related behaviors	Compulsive-addictive disorders
Loneliness	Confusion	Allergies	
Sadness	Hypervigilance		
Shame			
Guilt			
Numbness			

EMOTIONAL CHARACTERISTICS

While all ACoAs do not share the same mental, physical, or behavioral characteristics, they do, however, share the same underlying emotional states. These similar emotional states of being allow ACoAs to recognize and identify with each other, even though their behavior may be different. A good example of this is the ACoA who has a long string of unsuccessful relationships, and the ACoA who is "stuck" in a single relationship. For both of these ACoAs the root issue is most likely fear and distrust. One person acts out the fear and distrust by moving from relationship to relationship, and the other acts out the fear and distrust by staying in the same unhealthy relationship long after it is time to bail out. As these two ACoAs talk to each other, they find that, although their outer behavior is very dissimilar, their inner feelings are very similar.

When a group of ACoAs get together, they often feel immediate kinship with each other, regardless of which of the four types of alcoholic families they come from or how dissimilar their individual outer behavior has been.

Core Emotions

Looking at the chart, under the Emotional Characteristics heading, at the top of the list is fear. There is good reason for this. Fear is the root issue and core emotion of all ACoAs. The underlying fear is manifested in anger and hurt. The fear, anger, and hurt, along with resentment, distrust, sadness, and loneliness, have been discussed in detail in the previous chapter.

Although abandonment is a core experience for ACoAs, it is an oversimplification to state that abandonment and the emotional effects of abandonment are the only issues that have an emotional impact on the ACoA. The actions of the alcoholic, and the enforcement of the four family rules, discussed in previous sections, have a great impact on the child growing up in the alcoholic family. All of the above emotions—fear, anger, hurt, resentment, distrust, sadness, and loneliness—are emotional states that are a result of the irrational behavior of the alcoholic family.

These secondary emotional states are very painful to the ACoA, and must be resolved for true recovery to take place. Abandonment, however, must be dealt with as a major issue. If abandonment is not resolved, then recovery will be crippled. And recovery is possible.

Shame and Guilt

The alcoholic family is a system based on shame and guilt. The family uses shame and guilt to enforce the family rules. This shame and guilt should not be minimized. The ACoA must acknowledge and talk about the feelings of shame, guilt, and other painful emotions that are a direct result of the behavior of the alcoholic family. This is a must for recovery. In my experience, however, as the shame and guilt are talked about, this will lead to the core issues of fear, anger, and hurt.

Numbness

It is important to note that the way most ACoAs deal with painful emotional states is by "going numb." The ACoA, as he or she is growing up, learns very quickly that showing feelings is not okay. In order to survive all of the painful emotional states that develop as a result of the dynamics of the alcoholic family, the child learns to turn off feelings. Although the feelings may be turned off, that does not mean that they do not exist. ACoAs who talk about never feeling any strong emotions are like volcanoes: At any moment they have the potential to explode.

MENTAL CHARACTERISTICS

The ACoA develops a mental outlook and a way of looking at the world that is directly related to living in an alcoholic family. The rules governing the family shape the thoughts of the child growing up in the alcoholic system.

Thinking in Absolutes

ACoAs do not have a sense of the process of life. They think in terms of black or white and are generally unable to negotiate for their needs. In all areas of their lives it's all or nothing. This leads to being superresponsible or superirresponsible on the job and in other life situations.

Lack of Information

ACoAs as a rule do not possess concrete information on how to live life. When they were growing up, there was no one to answer their questions. When an AcoA says, "I don't know" or "I don't understand," it is not a lie. The lack of information is both in concrete knowledge and in the ability to deal with emotional states.

Compulsive Thinking

ACoAs often become focused on one thought or idea and cannot get this thought or idea out of their minds. The thought becomes compulsive. Even if the ACoA does not act on the thought, it still rules the thinking process. This obsessive thinking can be focused on a job, a person, or almost anything else in the ACoA's life.

Indecision

ACoAs often have trouble making decisions. They get caught between endlessly trying to figure out all the possibilities, and having to be perfect. Often the roots of indecision lie in an early-childhood parental divorce, where the child thinks that he or she has to make a decision between which parent to love. This is a no-win situation.

Learning Disabilities

ACoAs appear to have a high incidence of learning disabilities, such as dyslexia. Often these learning disabilities go undiscovered and cause the child a great deal of trouble in school.

Confusion

ACoAs often have difficulty in thinking clearly. Their thoughts are confused and muddled. Under pressure, the confusion becomes acute, and the ACoA sometimes becomes paralyzed and unable to act.

Hypervigilance

Some ACoAs are acutely aware of all the things that are going on around them. They need to be aware of everything that is happening in order to feel safe. This is a direct result of growing up in an unsafe environment, where they need to be aware of exactly what was happening so they would know how to act.

Although most ACoAs do not display all of these mental characteristics, most have at least one or more.

PHYSICAL CHARACTERISTICS

ACoAs often have a wide variety of physical disorders that are a result of growing up in an alcoholic family, which is a high-stress environment. These physical symptoms that occur in some ACoAs range from mild discomfort to severely disabling.

Tense Shoulders

ACoAs often carry their repressed feelings in their shoulders and upper back. The area around the upper shoulders where the shoulders and neck meet is often very hard and almost rocklike. This often causes headaches.

Lower Back Pain

ACoAs often display their feelings of lack of support and being isolated in their lower back. This can cause a dull ache or a sharp pain in the lower back region. Often the discomfort will be on one side or the other.

Sexual Dysfunction

ACoAs often obsess about sex to the point where they cannot function sexually, or withdraw from their sexuality and do not participate. Sexual dysfunction in ACoAs is not surprising, considering the high rate of sexual abuse in alcoholic families. This abuse includes not only girls; there is increasing evidence that a high percentage of boys have been sexually abused. The range of dysfunction is wide and often includes impotence, performance anxiety, inability to have orgasms, and deep feelings of shame or guilt, which make sex uncomfortable or impossible.

Gastro-intestinal Disorders

ACoAs often have a wide variety of intestinal disorders, such as ulcers, chronic constipation, diarrhea, chronic heartburn, and upset stomach. Repressed emotions often cause gastro-intestinal problems. There is a reason why "gut feelings" are called that. The repression of these feelings can cause disease.

Stress-related Disorders

ACoAs often have frequent colds and flus and have difficulty sleeping. A growing body of evidence also suggests that ACoAs get more than their share of cancer and other diseases. A feeling of fatigue and a general state of low energy are often a part of the ACoA's life.

Allergies

ACoAs often are allergic to foods, pollen, molds, and a host of other items, including alcohol and other drugs.

Many of the above diseases have direct links to the emotional effects of being raised in an alcoholic family. After ACoAs have been in treatment, many of their physical problems become resolved. It is important, however, to acknowledge that many of the illnesses of ACoAs can and should be treated by a qualified medical doctor. A good physical examination that includes allergy testing is not only desirable, but could be life-saving. Stomach problems can be caused by insufficient stomach acid which, in many cases, is easily remedied, if discovered. Low energy and fatigue can be caused by a variety of physical problems, including vitamin deficiency or adrenal fatigue. Whatever the problem, a physical exam should be a part of the recovery process.

BEHAVIORAL CHARACTERISTICS

There are certain behavioral characteristics and traits that ACoAs share. All ACoAs do not share the same characteristics, but they do share the same reasons for developing these traits. The behavioral characteristics of the ACoA were developed as a way of responding to the unpredictable and sometimes dangerous behavior of the alcoholic family. As a child grows up he or she has a tendency to model the behaviors of the parents and other important adults. Since the adults in the alcoholic family are acting in accordance with the four family rules, the child will also learn to behave in accordance with these rules.

The child in an alcoholic family will not only model the behavior of the adults in the family, but will also develop behaviors that are survival-oriented. Some of the behavioral characteristics that are common to ACoAs are described below.

Crisis-oriented Living

The nature of the alcoholic family is to live from one crisis to the next. The ACoA organizes his or her life in a way that insures that crises will occur on a regular basis. If a crisis does not happen, the ACoA will often create one. This crisis-oriented existence keeps the ACoA in a constant state of activity that helps the ACoA feel alive and useful. The constant activity also sets up a smoke screen so that the ACoA does not have time to take a serious look at him- or herself.

Manipulative Behavior

The ACoA has a desperate need to control his or her environment. This includes people, jobs, physical space, and just about anything else. This need to control is directly related to growing up in the unpredictable and emotionally immature alcoholic family. The child growing up in this family has a need to establish some consistency in his or her life. Since the alcoholic family is out of control, regardless of how it appears, the child in this system tries to control the system in order to bring about some consistency. Since the child's needs for love, affection, attention, and recognition cannot be met by the alcoholic family, the child will develop manipulative techniques in order to get his or her needs met. The ACoA, having learned as a child how to get his or her needs met, will continue to behave in a manipulative manner all of his or her life unless this pattern is recognized and broken. Thus, the ACoA does not know any other way to behave, but suspects that he or she is doing something that is unhealthy.

Intimacy Problems

Intimacy requires trust, communication, and the ability to resolve conflict. The ACoA has very little training on how to do any of these and learns at a very early age not to trust. The ACoA also has difficulty expressing feelings, talking about needs and wants, and sometimes even carrying on general conversation, let alone talking about things that are personally important. ACoAs are not able to resolve conflict. They would rather pretend that it does not exist; they cannot negotiate. The ACoA approaches relationships in two basic ways. First is the shotgun approach, in which the ACoA jumps from one relationship to another, seeking some unattainable magical quality in another person that will make him or her okay. The second is the bulldog approach, in which the ACoA finds one person and clings to him or her for dear life, no matter how sick or unwilling the other person is. The sad thing is that the ACoA knows that something is wrong with these kinds of relationships. However, the ACoA cannot quite figure out what it is. When asked what intimacy is, most ACoAs will get a blank look and give a confused answer.

Inability to Have Fun

The alcoholic family is so serious and chaotic that the children in the family never learn how to play. An alcoholic family is not a fun place to be. The inability to have fun is also linked to the need to control; it's hard to have fun when you're trying to control everything. Most ACoAs take everything very seriously. Even when they are laughing and appear to be having fun, they are waiting for the ax to fall and the fun to come to an abrupt, painful halt.

Trying to Fit In

Most ACoAs try to fit in with whatever group they happen to be in. They are masters at blending into crowds; regardless of how uncomfortable they feel inside, their outside tries to remain natural. ACoAs have a real fear of drawing attention to themselves. This is directly related to their roots in the alcoholic family, where it could be downright dangerous to draw attention to oneself. The fear of being noticed follows most ACoAs all of their lives.

Compulsive-addictive Behavior

The alcoholic family is a compulsive-addictive one, and the children from this system learn compulsive-addictive behaviors. I don't believe that there is any other group that is more compulsive and addictive than ACoAs. They learn this behavior as children and, without intervention, will continue it until they die. Compulsive and addictive behavior is extremely painful, and the range of behaviors is almost limitless. If it can be done, the ACoA will find a way to do it compulsively and addictively. Some of the more common behaviors include:

1. Alcoholism—the ACoA is a very high-risk candidate for the disease.

2. Drug addiction—as in alcoholism, the ACoA is at high risk.
3. Eating disorders such as overeating, anorexia, and bulimia.
4. Smoking.
5. Addictive relationships.
6. Addicted to and compulsive about sex.
7. Addicted and compulsive about exercise.
8. Compulsive about being perfect and doing a perfect job.
9. Addicted and compulsive about —— (fill in the blank; it could be just about anything).

The categorization of the ACoA's characteristics into the four main groupings of emotional, mental, physical, and behavioral is an attempt to clarify a syndrome that is extremely complex in nature. When viewing the above model, it is important to realize that the model is not the person. Each individual ACoA is unique. The common characteristics of ACoAs are a result of the shared experience of being raised in an alcoholic family. It is this shared experience, and the resulting emotional baseline of fear, anger, and hurt, that is the true common denominator. The mental, physical, and behavioral characteristics may change from person to person, but the emotional baseline is the same.

The ACoA is driven by internal forces and motives that, for the most part, are of an unconscious nature. ACoAs do not know why they feel, think, and behave as they do, and when they do gain insight into their feelings and behaviors, often do not believe that they can change. They feel stuck and hopeless. But ACoAs do recover, and have been recovering by the thousands; I have never run across a group of people who are more dedicated to recovery. Their courage and willingness is inspiring. In Part Two of this book techniques for recovery will be explored in depth.

7

Chronic Shock

The five-year-old boy sat in his room at his desk. He was staring into a coloring book and his crayons were laid neatly beside him, ready to fill the blank spaces between the lines with bright colors. His hands made no move to the colored crayons and his eyes did not really see the pages of the coloring book. Instead, he was listening to his mother and father fight—again.

The words of the fight were not clear, but he could hear the rise and fall of his parents' voices over the background noise of the TV. He was always afraid when his parents fought, and he always tried to make himself scarce whenever a fight broke out between them. This particular argument did not seem any different from any of the other arguments that his mom and dad had had in the past. Their fights always frightened him, and somehow he always felt that he was to blame.

Suddenly the tempo of the fight downstairs picked up, and he heard his father shout, "It's my house, and I'll do what the hell I want." He heard his mother scream something that sounded like "No." Then there was the loud crack of a gun being fired.

The house became absolutely quiet. The boy held his breath and listened for a sound—any sound. Fear seemed to grow and swell up inside of him. He wanted desperately to find out what had happened downstairs, but he was frozen in his chair. He just sat and stared blankly at his coloring book. After what seemed forever, he heard his mother sobbing. His first thought was She's alive, he didn't kill her.

After a time the boy began breathing again. He slid off his chair, went out of his room, and down the stairs. His heart was pounding as he came to the living-room door. As he looked into the living room he could see his father sitting in the chair in front of the TV. There was a drink in his father's hand, and a pistol lay smoking in his lap. The TV was silent and the screen was shattered where a bullet had smashed into it. His mother was sitting on the couch, crying. She looked up, saw him in the doorway, and said in an even voice, "Your father shot out the TV. Go to bed."

The little boy went back to his room and got undressed and climbed into bed. The house was quiet. Inside of the boy the overwhelming fear had turned into numbness. If the child were asked what he felt at this time, he would have said, "Nothing." He would not have been lying; he truly felt nothing. In later years he would look back at this incident and not feel any emotions. His memory would function as if he were watching a TV show, as if he were an observer of the event and not a participant.

In the above case history the child went into shock. The shock state was based upon the view of the child that one parent had killed another. For a child the loss—or the imagined loss—of one or both parents is a catastrophic event; the child is overwhelmed by fear. Children depend on their parents for their security, and in the above situation the child had been faced with the death of a parent.

During the shock state certain events happen to both the emotional and physical aspects of the person experiencing the shock. On the physical level the body gears itself up to manage the disaster. Some of the things that occur are:

1. The normal breathing patterns change. The person holds his breath during the initial phase of the shock and when breathing resumes, it is generally ragged and uneven.
2. Adrenaline is released into the system by the adrenal glands.

3. The heart rate quickens and the blood pressure elevates.
4. The person's eyes may appear vacant and distant.
5. The face may lose color and may appear grayish.
6. The skin may feel cold to the touch.

On the emotional level, the person shuts down, or becomes numb. In the above case history the child became numb because he was unable to deal with the overwhelming fear that one of his parents had been killed. We must keep in mind the child's point of view. Children cannot live without adults to take care of them. Young children do not have the skills to survive in the world without adults, and generally speaking, the only adults whom they know and trust are their parents. The death, or the imagined death, of a parent threatens both the emotional and physical existence of a child. Children know that they cannot survive by themselves. Going numb was a protective measure on the part of the child. He was protecting himself from the overwhelming fear of not only the loss of a parent, but the possibility of his not surviving the shooting. He went into shock.

Shock and recovery generally conform to the following model. First there is the reaction to the catastrophe—shock. This is when the initial psychological/physical effects of the trauma occur. Second is the rebound stage, when the feelings of the person experiencing the trauma or catastrophe begin to be felt. Third is the resolution stage, when the person resolves the feelings of fear, anger, loss, etc., that they were experiencing as a result of the initial trauma.

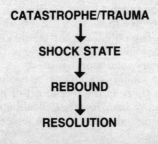

CATASTROPHE/TRAUMA

↓

SHOCK STATE

↓

REBOUND

↓

RESOLUTION

What happened to this boy during, and immediately after, the shooting incident was that at the time of the shooting, he went into shock. His emotions shut down. A part of him that expressed his feelings was repressed, and he went numb. While the shutting down of emotions is normal in the shock state, this boy never fully recovered; he never had a chance to process his feelings and part of him stayed numb. A piece of his emotional life was repressed. All through the boy's life, through his teen years, and into adulthood, a part of the boy would remain in shock. This is chronic shock. Restated, chronic shock is the experiencing of a catastrophic event, and not resolving the physical/psychological effects of that catastrophe. Many ACoAs, because of the inherent nature of the alcoholic family, suffer from chronic shock.

The situation described above is a true case history. What must be remembered is that the incident described was but one in a series of incidents. That is true for many children who come from alcoholic families. Growing up in an alcoholic family can be a series of trauma/shock/repressions.

Trauma and stress are a part of the human condition. All of us learn how to deal with events in our lives that are traumatic and painful. The success with which we deal with these events to a large extent determines how full our emotional lives will be. The child who was raised in an alcoholic family learns to deal with the traumas of life in a way that helps him survive, but this does not release this child from the emotional effects of the trauma.

The alcoholic family operates in a mode that is dysfunctional. The four family rules of rigidity, silence, denial, and isolation insure that if there is a traumatic event, the event will not be resolved in a healthy way. The alcoholic family cannot resolve these issues in a healthy way; it does not know how. The only thing the family knows how to do is become more rigid, more silent, deny that anything is out of the ordinary, and more isolated.

The alcoholic family is a chaotic and often violent system. Therefore there is the likelihood of more trauma in an alcoholic family than in other, healthier families. The drug, when consumed, often leads to violent behavior and increases the likelihood of serious accidents. Therefore there is an increased possibility that ACoAs will suffer from chronic shock. In fact, my conservative estimate would be that over 50% of those raised in alcoholic families are to some degree in chronic shock.

In the healthy family system the child has an opportunity to process his or her feelings and get emotional resolution to whatever caused the trauma. This resolution may take time and work on the part of the parents and the child, but it does happen.

The loving support and safety that a child needs to resolve traumatic issues does not exist in the alcoholic family. The alcoholic family is not a safe place for a child.

The Chronic Shock Flowchart on page 54 graphically points out the difference between how a child from an alcoholic family and a child from a healthy family deal with a shock event. Let's look a little more closely, reading from the top down.

The Child

The human organism seeks to remain in homeostasis, or balance. This balance insures that there is a consistent and stable environment for the organism, which in this case is the child. Even when the child is living in an alcoholic family—no matter how dysfunctional the family —the child has found some kind of internal balance and has arranged some kind of stability to aid his survival.

Shock Event

This is the catastrophic event that has severely upset the child's balance. The event could be the death of a parent, or, as in the previous case history, the imagined death of a parent. The event could also be any type of sexual abuse, a physical trauma such as surgery, or an accident. Divorce, the breakup of the family, and child abuse—both verbal and physical—can also be shock events. The list is not limited to the above.

Chronic Shock Flowchart

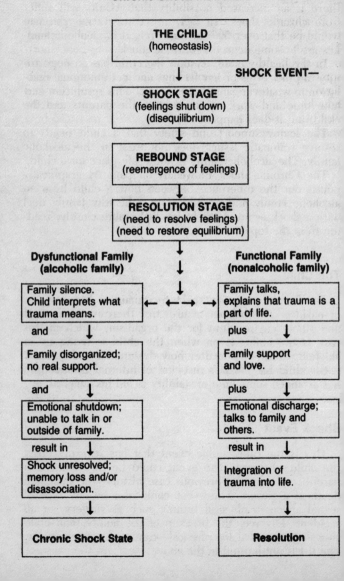

Shock Stage

During this stage the physical and emotional effects of the trauma are felt; the human organism is on overload. The body gears up for the disaster—rapid heartbeat, shortness of breath, and adrenaline entering the system are some of the physical events that occur. Emotional shutdown occurs; the person experiences being numb. If asked how he felt, the person would most likely answer that he was okay and did not feel anything. There may also be a vacant or distant look in his or her eyes.

Rebound Stage

It is in this stage that the person—in this case a child—begins to seek to restore himself to the preshock state. At this time the physical body begins to rebalance itself, and the emotions that have been shut down begin to be felt. The person has a desire and a need to talk about the shock event.

Resolution Stage

In this stage the person experiencing the trauma resolves the feelings which he or she had about the catastrophe. The fear, anger, terror, hurt, rage, hopelessness, and helplessness that are experienced are talked about and resolved. Equilibrium is restored to the person. Not only is the shock resolved, but during resolution the person learns and grows from the catastrophic event. Until the resolution stage there is little difference between how the child of an alcoholic family reacts and how the child from a healthy family reacts. Let's look more closely at the differences between what takes place in the alcoholic family and what takes place in a healthy, functional family.

Functional Family

It is explained that trauma is a part of life and that it can happen to anyone. The child gains a realistic view of the event, and understands that he or she is not the cause of

the catastrophe. The family provides emotional support
and safety. The child is then able to express the overwhelming feelings that occur during the shock state.

The child is able to discharge the emotions that he has
stored up in his body. The openness and ability to talk,
not just to family members, but also to those outside the
family, such as counselors, school personnel, and friends,
is extremely important. This allows the child to integrate
the incident into his life. When this integration is complete, the shock is healed and resolution is achieved. The
child is whole and healthy.

Alcoholic Family

There is a marked difference in how the child living in an
alcoholic family deals with trauma. In the alcoholic family
silence engulfs the members; no one talks about the incident. The child is left to interpret what the trauma means.
This interpretation often takes the form of the child blaming
himself for the occurrence of the traumatic event. He is
unable to talk about his emotions to anyone in the family.
This silence also extends outside of the family. One of the
rules of the alcoholic family is the rule of silence, and
during a catastrophic event this rule is in full force. The
child has no one to turn to, no one who is safe enough for
him to express those feelings that are bottled up inside.
The members may appear to pull together and support
one another, but this is an illusion. In reality the alcoholic
family is disorganized and provides very little support.

As a result of being unable to talk and express the
feelings that are inside of him and without the support of
the family, the child shuts down emotionally. A part of the
child becomes numb and stays that way. The overwhelming fear that the child has as a result of the trauma must be
dealt with, and he will deal with it any way he can. At this
point memory loss often occurs, and the child loses the
ability to recall the event. The child may also dissociate
from the event, and although he may be able to recall the
trauma, when it is remembered, it is as if it happened to
another person. The child will often relate that the memory of the trauma has a movielike quality. This dissociation

and memory loss will extend into adulthood, and until treated, will remain with the person. When the shock is not resolved, the Chronic Shock State occurs.

Case History

At twenty-six Lisa R. joined an ACoAs group. She presented many of the same problems that ACoAs seem to have in abundance. She felt that she was not normal, she feared and wanted intimacy, and she felt she did not have the skills to make it in the world. She was fearful that she would never have a full emotional life. Anytime she was faced with a stressful ("good or bad") situation, she went numb. Lisa knew that going numb was not normal, but this was a pattern she had adopted all of her life.

During group therapy it was revealed that Lisa had been sexually molested when she was five years old by a nonfamily member, a stranger. When Lisa spoke of the molestation, she was unemotional—as if it had happened to someone else. She could remember that the event had taken place, but could not remember any of the details. In her words "It is as if four or five hours have been ripped out of my life."

Although Lisa's parents found out about the molestation, nothing therapeutic was done for their daughter. She was told to forget about what had happened and not to talk about it. Because of the already established "no talk" rules in Lisa's alcoholic family, she was not able to resolve any of the feelings that she had about being molested. The ring of silence that bound Lisa's family also extended outside the bounds of the immediate family. Consequently Lisa could not get outside support from anyone.

Using the Chronic Shock Flowchart on page 54, it is easy to see why Lisa went into chronic shock. As you study Lisa's chart below, compare the differences between her real family situation and the hypothetical healthy family situation.

It is important for ACoAs to understand these effects, because so many ACoAs are in chronic shock. When an ACoA feels stuck or unable to move in recovery, very often it is the chronic-shock issue that is hampering the recov-

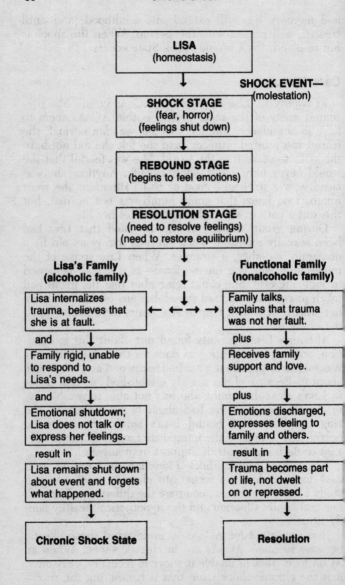

LISA
(homeostasis)

SHOCK EVENT—
(molestation)

SHOCK STAGE
(fear, horror)
(feelings shut down)

REBOUND STAGE
(begins to feel emotions)

RESOLUTION STAGE
(need to resolve feelings)
(need to restore equilibrium)

Lisa's Family
(alcoholic family)

Functional Family
(nonalcoholic family)

Lisa internalizes
trauma, believes that
she is at fault.

Family talks,
explains that trauma
was not her fault.

and

plus

Family rigid, unable
to respond to
Lisa's needs.

Receives family
support and love.

and

plus

Emotional shutdown;
Lisa does not talk or
express her feelings.

Emotions discharged,
expresses feeling to
family and others.

result in

result in

Lisa remains shut down
about event and forgets
what happened.

Trauma becomes part
of life, not dwelt
on or repressed.

Chronic Shock State

Resolution

ery process. The problem is that unless the ACoA, or his or her therapist, knows about chronic shock, they will miss the issue altogether. Counselors of ACoAs will have so many clients in chronic shock, that if the therapists don't have some understanding of it, they will be able to assist their clients only so far in the recovery process. Until chronic-shock issues are resolved, there will be only limited recovery, which, of course, is better than no recovery at all.

An ACoA may choose not to work on chronic-shock issues. If this is the case, it does not mean that the ACoA will not make progress. Many people choose not to resolve chronic-shock issues; they experience limited recovery and are at peace with that. Ricki, an ACoA who was in a therapy group of mine, is a good example of a person who chose not to work on a chronic-shock issue. She had been in therapy for approximately one year and had done excellent work on becoming more assertive in her relationships with men. This was the primary reason that she entered therapy. In the course of therapy it came to light that she had an older brother who had been killed in an automobile accident when she was five years old. She had only vague memories of him, but had a feeling that she and he were very close. She also had very sketchy memories of that period of time in her life.

When I asked her about how her family dealt with her brother's death, her reply was "That was a subject that no one ever talked about. I think I remember that my mother cleaned out his room and packed his stuff away, but I'm not sure; we just never brought his name up in family conversation again. He was gone, and no one talked about it." When Ricki talked about her brother, her voice filled with emotion and she got teary-eyed.

I talked to her about chronic shock and told her that if she decided to work on this issue, she would most likely experience the grief and loss that she was unable to process when she was a child. I also told her that, on the positive side, the releasing of the blocked emotions of grief and loss might positively change the difficulty she had in allowing herself to become more open and vulnerable in intimate relationships with men. Ricki chose not to work on the issue. She did not wish to "open up a Pandora's box." She was content with the work that she had done and thought that maybe someday in the future she would be willing to work on the death of her brother. I supported her decision. No one should ever be forcefully encouraged to work on issues that he or she does not want to work on.

Symptoms of Chronic Shock

Below are some of the symptoms that ACoAs can look for to determine if they are in chronic shock. Self-diagnosing chronic shock can be very helpful to the ACoA's recovery process. However, as with most self-diagnosis, it is often desirable to check your conclusions with a qualified professional counselor. It is important that ACoAs have information about chronic shock so that they can determine whether they wish to proceed with treatment. (This section was also written with the therapist in mind, and was designed to assist the therapist in identifying clients who are in chronic shock.)

1. A narrow range of emotional experience.

This generally manifests in two distinct types. The first is the person who feels he or she has been short-changed in the emotions department. This person feels that his or her emotions are not deep, and has a sense that he or she is not experiencing a full range of emotions. Sometimes he or she will state that he doesn't feel anything deeply. These individuals do very often, however, experience emotional outbursts like fits of rage and deep unexplained grief. The second type is the person who may appear to have deep emotions, and he or she does, but the range of emotional experience is narrow. These individuals swing between anger, sadness, terror, and fear, but they don't experience the broad range of emotions that is possible in the human experience.

2. A feeling of going numb when faced with talking about a painful experience.

ACoAs have learned how to survive, and one of the most effective survival techniques is going numb, or shutting down emotionally. When faced with the overwhelming emotional pain of trauma, ACoAs unconsciously block emotions and do not feel. When, during therapy, they are faced with talking about the painful periods in their lives, where one or more catastrophic traumas happened, ACoAs will go numb. This is unconscious and is their way of protecting themselves. This learned way of dealing with painful events is something at which ACoAs are masters, and they use it on almost any occasion when they feel they are being pressed or overwhelmed. Unfortunately ACoAs often go numb during happy or overwhelming events, such as weddings.

3. Poor or no memory recall of the time surrounding a traumatic event.

Another way that ACoAs deal with overwhelming trauma is to repress the memory of the event. Many times they will have a sense that something important has happened to them, but they cannot remember what it was. Generally speaking, the more violent or repressive the alcoholic family was, the greater the memory loss. Holidays can be very stressful and violent in the alcoholic family. Many times the existence of trauma can be discovered when ACoAs try to remember their holiday experiences.

4. Shortened attention span.

This is another way to avoid reexperiencing the trauma. When asked about a particular traumatic event, ACoAs in chronic shock will often refocus on another topic. During therapy they will unconsciously do this over and over. The closer they get to the event, the more they will attempt to change the topic.

5. Confused thinking.

Another way to mask trauma is by confused thinking, which is caused by the overwhelming fear that is felt as a result of the trauma. When ACoAs begin to reexperience the emotional impact of the catastrophic event, their thought patterns can become very disjointed and disorganized. This confusion allows ACoAs to avoid dealing with the emotional effects of the event. Confused thinking keeps ACoAs in their heads and away from their feelings.

6. A feeling of hopelessness.

When faced with an overwhelming catastrophe, a feeling that "this will never end" and "there is no hope that things will get better" is manifested. When the shock of the event is not resolved, this feeling of hopelessness remains with the person. It is common to hear ACoAs speak of their hopelessness.

7. A feeling of helplessness.

Because of the nature of the catastrophic events that cause chronic shock, it is natural for the person involved to feel helpless, both during and immediately after the event has taken place. For those suffering from chronic shock the feeling of helplessness remains with them. It manifests in all areas of their lives, including relationships and work situations. A common statement or attitude that ACoAs in chronic shock share is "There is nothing that I or anyone else can do to help me feel better or more whole."

8. Many times the ACoA who is in chronic shock will identify joy or happiness as the absence of painful emotions rather than as a feeling itself.

9. Intense feelings at inappropriate times.

These are feelings, directly linked to the shock event that have gone unresolved and will continue to surface until the shock is resolved. ACoAs in chronic shock have these feelings bottled up inside of them and cannot control when they will surface. Some of the most common feelings are intense grief, anger, and sadness. These feelings seem to come up for no apparent reason, and may be triggered by movies, TV shows, etc. ACoAs do not know where these feelings come from, and they are mystified as to why they have them.

10. Denying that a traumatic event has had any effect.

ACoAs very often make statements like "I remember Dad tearing the phone off the wall and hitting Mom with it, but I don't think that has had any effect on me" or "It was no big deal." The truth is that the event did make a big impact on them, but they are not capable of recognizing that because they have repressed the emotional impact of the occurrence.

11. Observation during therapy.

During therapy sessions ACoAs will often display the physical characteristics of a person in shock. This happens most often when the counselor begins to explore the time in the client's life when the catastrophic event occurred. When I worked as a counselor in the emergency room of a city hospital, I received much firsthand experience in working with people who had experienced extreme shock. During therapy sessions in private practice I noticed that people who had experienced a trauma in their past that was unresolved—and even unremembered—often reexperienced the physical as well as the emotional characteristics of shock victims (i.e., rapid heartbeat, ragged breath patterns, look of horror, feeling cold, etc.).

The counselor who chooses to work with ACoAs must have not only a firm basis in general counseling skills and principles, but must also have a wide range of knowledge in dealing with specific issues such as incest, sexual abuse of all kinds, child abuse (both physical and emotional), unresolved grief, and catastrophic trauma. All of the above can individually or collectively cause chronic shock. Due to the very nature of the alcoholic family with its high stress and tendency toward violence and abuse of all kinds, the ACoAs population is at a much higher risk than the general population to be in chronic shock.

When I facilitate ACoAs groups, each having no more than seven people, I can count on having at least one person who was sexually abused as a child, one who had a parent die, one who suffered physical abuse, and one or more whose parents divorced in a traumatic way. I can also count on these people being in chronic shock because

they have not been able to reach resolution on any of
these issues.

Treating Chronic Shock

Since the treatment for chronic shock almost always
involves a professional counselor, I have written this section to assist the therapist in designing treatment strate-
gies for clients who are in chronic shock. Therefore much
of the text is worded with the counselor-client relationship
in mind. Those ACoAs who read this, and who are not
counselors, are encouraged to use this information to assess, for themselves, if they are in chronic shock, and
then, if appropriate, to seek professional treatment.

When treating ACoAs who are in chronic shock, it is
important to be aware that there is a general order or flow
to the treatment. Once we are aware that the chronic-
shock state exists, the ACoA can be guided through the
stages of treatment. These stages are diagrammed in the
Treatment Flowchart. We will continue to use Lisa's case
history as a model. We can do this because even though
there is a difference between each client, and a difference
in the kind of situations that cause chronic shock, the
generalized treatment is basically the same in all cases.
Although the cycles of treatment are generally the same,
the length of treatment will vary greatly from person to
person.

Let's look more closely at the Treatment Flowchart.

I. Chronic-shock State

This is the cycle of unexplained feelings, emotional shut-
downs, and unexplainable behaviors that are linked to the
shock event (see previous definition for more detail). In
Lisa's case these symptoms were being unable to experience her feelings (going numb), unreasonable fear about
being alone, sexual dysfunction, and the inability to become intimate with men.

Treatment Flowchart

I.	**CHRONIC-SHOCK STATE**	Cycles of unexplained feelings, emotional shutdowns, and unexplained behaviors that are linked to the shock event.
and		
II.	**NEED TO RESOLVE**	Awareness on the part of the client that something is amiss in his or her life and a desire to change.
and		
III.	**THERAPEUTIC ENVIRONMENT**	Safe place to experience the feelings repressed at the time of the trauma; creates a healthy family atmosphere.
plus		
IV.	**CYCLES OF REEXPERIENCE**	Client cycles in and out of the shock experience, feeling emotions and shutting down.
plus		
V.	**EMOTIONAL DISCHARGE**	Feeling emotions that were repressed at the time of the trauma; release of pain and fear.
result in		
VI.	**SENSE OF RELEASE**	Increasing awareness of how the trauma has affected all aspects of life.
result in		
VII.	**RESOLUTION/ INTEGRATION**	Trauma becomes integrated as part of life experience.

II. Need to Resolve

As Lisa grew older and became more mature, she beg.
to have an increasing awareness that something was wro
with her. She did not know what was happening, but s
did know that she was not happy. When she enter
therapy, she said it was "to do something," but she did n
know what. She had tried to think her way into happine
and act her way into happiness, but it always eluded he
She was tired of trying and wanted to resolve what w
going on with her so she could be happy.

III. Therapeutic Environment

In order to work through chronic shock issues, th
client must have a safe environment. This is a *must*. Th
key element in providing a safe environment is trust. Th
client must develop a trusting relationship with the cou
selor, and if working in a group setting, trusting relatio
ships with the other group members. Building trust tak
time. It does not happen overnight; it is a process. Ta
time: Don't rush into deep emotional work prematurel
Before ACoAs can experience repressed emotions in fro
of others, they must take the essential step of trustin
that, unlike their alcoholic family of origin, the group w
not reject them from expressing their fear, anger, hur
rage, and shame. It is more than a coincidence that th
safe therapeutic environment is similar to the enviro
ment of the healthy family (see Chronic Shock Flowcha
on page 54). The person working through chronic-sho
issues will be experiencing some powerful and frightenin
emotions that have been repressed for a long time. Th
reason for chronic shock was that there was no safe pla
to work out powerful and frightening emotions. For Lisa
took several months in group for her to feel comfortab
and safe enough to begin to work on the issue of bei
molested.

V. Cycles of Reexperience

During this stage of treatment the client experiences the emotions and sometimes the physical effects of the original trauma. In this phase the client will typically dip into the experience and then shut down emotionally. Then he or she will dip back down into the experience and shut down again emotionally. This will occur again and again and is to be expected. ACoAs are masters at shutting down, and this is how they will attempt to deal with the feelings that they are experiencing. Normally it will take more than one or two sessions to work through a chronic-shock issue. It is a process that may take months to complete, particularly when working in a group setting. Lisa's recovery from chronic shock took months and required a number of individual sessions in addition to group work.

V. Emotional Discharge

The client in chronic shock has intense and deep emotions that have been repressed for a long time, sometimes decades and longer. As these emotions are experienced and recognized for what they are, the energy behind these emotions is discharged. It is the discharging of this energy that releases the client from the effects of chronic shock. When discharge takes place, healing can occur. Emotional discharge often takes place through catharsis: Sobbing, screaming in anger and rage, and screaming in fear are some of the ways this happens. Not all emotional discharge is cathartic. Many times discharge will take place quietly, with a quiet shudder or a tightening or relaxing of the body, accompanied by a sigh. Talking about the feelings that are being experienced is an important part of the process of discharging. As Lisa worked through her chronic shock she demonstrated all of the above types of discharge and release. This is true for most people who work through chronic-shock issues.

VI. Sense of Release

As the process of releasing and letting go of the pent-up feelings continues, many clients report that they feel lighter and looser. They often say that they feel free. This feeling of freedom is often accompanied by a heightened sense of self-awareness, an increase in the general level of health, and a more positive outlook on life. As Lisa continued her work her facial features became softer and less rigid. She reported that she felt less stuck and made some major changes in her relationships, both at work and in her personal life.

VII. Resolution/Integration

In this, the final phase, the shock event that was repressed has lost its power over the client and has been integrated into the client's life. It has become a part of his or her life experience, to be neither dwelt upon nor ignored. It often occurs during this phase that the catastrophic event that caused so much pain becomes a vehicle by which the client grows both emotionally and spiritually. At the time of this writing Lisa was becoming increasingly more aware of how her experience could become an asset and a powerful vehicle for her spiritual growth.

Some general guidelines that we can use when working with clients who are experiencing chronic shock are:

A.   Be aware that the condition exists, take in-depth client histories, being alert for the events that can cause chronic shock. This is very important. Taking a good solid history can shorten the client's time in therapy by helping the therapist focus on the important issues.

B.   Inform the client of what you know about chronic shock and how you will be working with it. It is important that the client know why he is feeling and behaving in a way that makes no logical sense and why there are chunks of memories missing from his life. It affirms that he is not crazy or odd; his life begins to make sense. An educated client is the most powerful ally a therapist can have.

C. Assist the client in filling in the memory gaps and remembering the details of the event. Encourage him to go and talk to family members and others who can be of assistance in filling in the lost parts of his personal history. During therapy encourage the client to recall the blocked memories. Remember to be patient and take as much time as is needed. Working to assist clients in getting their memories back is like putting together a jigsaw puzzle. It takes time to fit pieces together, and then all of a sudden the pattern becomes clear and suddenly the puzzle is complete and recognizable.

D. Challenge the denial. Most clients will try, unconsciously, to deny that the event ever happened, or that if it did happen, then it did not have very much impact on them. Challenging is the gentle art of reminding the client that whatever it was that happened to them has had a tremendous impact on their lives, both at the time the event took place and in the present. Very rarely is it necessary or desirable to use hard confrontation with clients in chronic shock.

E. Support and encourage the client through the feelings of hopelessness and helplessness. When the client is at the bottom of the pit of hopelessness and helplessness, it seems that things will never get better. They adopt the mind set of "What is the use of all of this?" It is very important to affirm to the client that the feelings that he is having are a part of the process of letting go of the trauma, that it is important to reexperience the repressed and blocked feelings in order to let go of them.

F. Do not push the client into moving too fast. Dealing with these issues takes time. Pushing can cause both physical and emotional damage to the client. Many

of the traumas of ACoAs involve physical abuse
either sexual or beatings or both. Remember tha
the original event was so overwhelming to the clien
that he or she repressed the emotional impact of it
remembering the event can and will be very pain
ful. Pushing the client too fast can result in actua
physical illness and emotional overload. A good rule
of thumb is "When in doubt, move slower."

G. If the client is a recovering alcoholic he or she mus
    have a firm basis in sobriety before working on these
    issues, which are highly charged emotionally and car
    cause much discomfort when they are being released
    The newly sober alcoholic or other chemically depen
    dent person generally needs some time to gain the
    emotional stability that is important to have in orde
    to work on chronic-shock issues.

H. Working in a group testing with ACoAs is a very
    effective method of dealing with these issues. The
    group not only gives much-needed support to the
    client, but also allows the individual work to be inter
    mittent rather than continuous. This spreads the worl
    out over a period of time and is potentially less
    debilitating to the client.

I. Chronic shock can happen at any age. Although the
    focus here has been on childhood, it is important to
    realize that chronic shock can occur whenever trauma
    is not resolved.

Working through chronic-shock issues is both painfu
and frightening. There is no way around this. ACoAs whe
are in chronic shock must be informed that the process o
recovery will hurt, but that at the end of the tunnel o
pain and fear there is freedom and joy that must be
experienced and understood. This is an act of faith or
the part of the adult child, faith and trust in us a
counselors, and in a broader sense faith in the proces
of the universe.

Dealing with the trauma of life is fundamentally a spiri

tual issue. The questions raised by adult children about why this happened to them will challenge not only the ACoAs beliefs and philosophies, but also those of the counselor.

PART TWO

·

RECOVERY
The Family Integration System

8
Recovery: A Process

Adult children of alcoholics can and do recover. Thousands of ACoAs are in the recovery process right now, and thousands more will be joining that process as more and more information about alcoholism and its effects on the family becomes available to the public. It must be remembered, however, that recovery is a process, not an event. Recovery is a way of living, a quality of feeling, and a mental attitude. Every ACoA who reads this has begun the recovery process. If you had not started this process, you would not be reading this. The recovery process for ACoAs begins with the realization—or sometimes just a suspicion—that their lives are not progressing in a way that is healthy.

Many ACoAs have this suspicion long before they find out what the problem is. Just the knowing that something is amiss is enough for the recovery process to start. Up until a few years ago ACoAs floundered around, moving from therapist to therapist, from self-help group to self-help group, trying this and that, never quite finding a solution to what was bothering them. This is still true in many parts of the country, but it is beginning to change. ACoA groups are springing up all over the country. Treatment for ACoAs is an idea whose time has come.

Central to the treatment and the recovery process for ACoAs is the knowledge that the source of the problem was being raised in an alcoholic family. This is the piece of information that was missing when ACoAs would go hither and yon, trying to discover what was wrong with them.

With this fact the action part of treatment can begin. It is important to restate that recovery is a process, and this process begins with a sense of unrest, pain, and a desire for a solution. The process never really ends; each ACoA in recovery keeps getting better and better.

In recovery the ACoA loses the deep sense of fear that is always with him or her. The anger and hurt lose their potency, and a true sense of happiness and joy can be experienced. This does not mean that recovery equals no problems or pain. What recovery does mean is that the ACoA becomes much better at dealing with life's bumps and crunches in a way that is healthier and healthier. The further along in the recovery process, the more adept the ACoA becomes in dealing with adversity. There is no graduation, but there is a sense of wonder and joy that goes hand in hand with recovery.

Recovery and health are a state of generally feeling good, not an absence of pain. ACoAs know what the absence of pain is—they have been going numb for years. That's how they learn to control the deep well of pain that they always carry around inside them.

The integrated recovery process for ACoAs has three primary components. For recovery to occur all three of these components must be addressed by the ACoA:

1. Emotional Discharge
2. Cognitive Reconstruction
3. Behavioral Action

These three components are interactive, and work in one area affects the other areas.

As can be seen in this chart, any work in one area affects the other areas. If the ACoA is doing emotional-discharge work, then the component of cognitive reconstruction will be affected, along with behavioral action. These areas cannot be separated. There is, however, a tendency for some people to concentrate in one area. If this happens, even though work in one area causes positive change in all areas, recovery will be lopsided and unidimensional. For recovery to proceed at an even pace all areas must be consciously addressed. Each person is different, and often

Interactive Recovery Process Chart

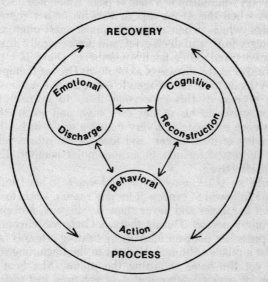

one person may feel more comfortable working in one area rather than another. There is nothing wrong with this as long as the ACoA is aware that all three areas must be addressed.

Let's look more closely at the three components of recovery.

Emotional Discharge

ACoAs are full of repressed emotions. They have carried these emotions around with them for years, and these must find a way out. They must be felt in order for the ACoA to let go and be free. We have seen in earlier sections of this book how the fear, anger, hurt, and other painful, harmful feelings were both developed and repressed. The four rules of the alcoholic family—silence, rigidity, isolation, and denial—insure that the ACoA will not be able to let go of these feelings.

For recovery the ACoA must find a way to purge himself

or herself of these repressed emotions. Until this happens, the ACoA will remain in a state of pain. Emotional discharge occurs when the ACoA experiences his or her repressed feelings, which, when released, appear most often as anger, rage, hurt, and deep grief, and are generally directed at parents and other family members. There is often a deep anger at the disease of alcoholism. During therapy the ACoA needs to be encouraged to express the emotions that were repressed; this expression leads to release. Each person works in his or her own way, and some ACoAs experience catharsis in a very emotive way—with a lot of displaying of hurt, anger, and fear—while others release their repressed feelings in a more quiet manner. Either way is effective.

Carla, an ACoA, never expressed anger. In her family no one was allowed to express it for any reason. Carla learned to stuff her anger and never show it. She was, however, a very angry person. During therapy Carla was encouraged to express her pent-up feelings by beating a tennis racket against a pillow. Although hesitant in the beginning, Carla soon got the hang of hitting the pillow. She beat that pillow for over twenty minutes—I got tired just watching her—and years of repressed anger came out. After the experience Carla told her ACoA therapy group that she had not felt this good in years.

In this example the repressed emotion was anger; it could just as easily have been hurt or grief. Whatever the repressed emotion, for recovery to occur it must be released and experienced.

Cognitive Reconstruction

Cognitive reconstruction is the process of learning how to think in a way that is healthy and acquiring a base of information about life. There are two main areas of the cognitive reconstruction process. First, ACoAs have a lack of information about living skills. No one was there for the ACoA to ask when he or she was growing up. There were no good teachers. ACoAs often do not know the practical aspects of living: how to negotiate with others, how to go about resolving conflict with others, how to use interpersonal-relationship skills. This is not surprising when the behavior of the alcoholic family is examined. These living skills can be learned, and they need to be. They are a critical part of the recovery process.

An ACoA named Ralph had great difficulty in asserting himself. He was afraid to draw attention to himself. When he was growing up, he found out that it was easier for him to be silent and not ask for anything since asking for something in his home could mean getting hurt. Consequently Ralph never learned that he could ask for what he wanted. This inability to ask extended into all areas of his life. For example, when Ralph went to eat in a restaurant, if he did not like the food or if he got the wrong order, he would not say anything to the waiter or waitress. In an intimate relationship he could not ask for emotional support, and could not tell his partner what he wanted sexually. The above are just two examples of many. During group therapy Ralph's major work was to tell the group what his needs were and then learn how to ask for what he wanted. He was quite successful in doing this. All he needed was to learn how to assert himself.

The second area of cognitive reconstruction is replacing the old tapes that ACoAs have about themselves. ACoAs have preprogrammed thoughts about who they are and how they are supposed to behave. These thoughts were implanted in their unconsciousness by the alcoholic family, and produced a limiting and negative view of themselves and of life in general. It is important for the ACoA to replace the negative programming with a more realistic and positive way of thinking. This is easier said than done; the negative programming of the ACoA is very deep. It is important for the ACoA to learn to use affirmations and positive-thinking techniques. These tools will assist the ACoA in reconstruction of his or her thinking. Later in this book affirmations and their use will be explained more fully.

Behavioral Action

Behavioral action is the process of the ACoA beginning to behave in a way that promotes a healthy life-style. In other words the ACoA is beginning to take care of himself or herself. The ACoA can begin to eat good healthy foods, to exercise, and generally to begin to live life in a healthy way. The ACoA must begin to modify behavior. Continuing to act in ways that are still sick will continue to keep the ACoA sick. The ACoA must begin to surround him- or herself with people who are themselves somewhere in the recovery process. This kind of support is invaluable.

The ACoA is often stuck in unhealthy relationships with parents, spouses, children, friends, and with people in the workplace. Movement toward health in these relationships often requires an actual change in behavior on the part of the ACoA—not just talk. This is very frightening for most ACoAs. They don't like change (rule number one, rigidity), but change is necessary. ACoAs must learn how to establish boundaries and how to set limits in relationships. These limits must then be acted upon.

Kim is an excellent example of behavioral action. She was in an emotionally and physically abusive relationship. She had worked on getting in touch with her feelings of anger and hurt, and had worked on discharging these feelings. She had also learned about the battered woman's syndrome, and was also in the process of using affirmations to restructure her thoughts. But she still felt that she could not get out of the relationship; she was afraid to be alone. Finally she took action, and although full of fear and with grave reservations, she physically removed herself from that abusive relationship. After refusing to see or talk to her ex-lover for a few weeks, she began to feel better and was able to see how stuck she had been. Kim had to act—in spite of her fears and what her old programming was telling her.

It is important to restate that the above three components of recovery must be interactive for recovery to progress in a balanced way. An ACoA who just focuses on behavioral action runs the risk of continuing to stuff feelings, and remains with a negative outlook on life. Those who work only on emotional discharge often get caught in reliving emotional crises again and again, without really letting go of the emotional pain. They continue to remain in relationships that are sick and harmful, and their outlook on life really does not change. Those who just work on being positive risk becoming Pollyannas who repress emotions and smile a lot, even though they are in emotional pain. They often remain in destructive situations, and try to think their way out of them.

The Recovery Process Chart is a model for recovery.

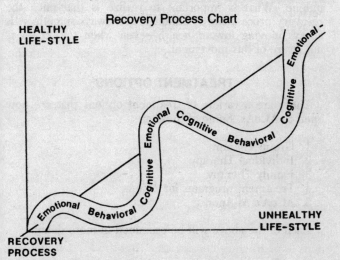

Recovery Process Chart

HEALTHY
LIFE-STYLE

Emotional *Behavioral* *Cognitive* *Emotional* *Cognitive* *Behavioral* *Cognitive* *Emotional*

UNHEALTHY
LIFE-STYLE

RECOVERY
PROCESS

In the Recovery Process Chart the healthy life-style bar on the left represents a recovery life-style where the ACoA has reconstructed all components of his or her life into a mode that supports physical, emotional, mental, and spiritual well-being. The unhealthy life-style bar on the bottom of the chart represents following the repressive rules of the alcoholic family. The recovery process bar in the middle represents growth toward a healthy life-style. The ACoA is represented by the cycle bar that cycles above and below the recovery process bar in the middle.

Looking at the chart above, it is apparent that the recovery process for the ACoA is a continual series of peaks and valleys. Recovery is not a smooth, even process. The ACoA will experience times of intense work and times of less intensity. This is normal. The ACoA often interprets the down cycle as being stuck. Most times this is not true, and the ACoA will get out of it.

The cycles themselves consist of the three components of recovery: emotional discharge, cognitive reconstruction, and behavioral action. There is no particular order to this process. Each ACoA will find a cycle and order that is unique. What is important to realize is that once the recovery process starts, although not always smooth, it is always moving toward health—even when the ACoA is not aware of this movement.

TREATMENT OPTIONS

There are a variety of treatment options that are now open to ACoAs. Some of these are:

1. Group Therapy
2. Individual Therapy
3. Family Therapy
4. Treatment programs for ACoAs
5. ACoA's Al-Anon

Each of the above will be examined in more detail.

Group Therapy

Although group therapy has been around for some time, it has only been in the last few years that some therapy groups have focused specifically on ACoA issues. An ACoA therapy group can be an important component of the recovery process. In the group setting, with a skilled facilitator, the ACoA can begin to break the four rules of the alcoholic family and learn to interact with other people in a way that is healthy. Becoming a part of a healthy group is an important part of the recovery process for ACoAs. Generally groups can be divided into two main categories: information groups and process groups.

Information groups focus on providing concrete information to the ACoA about the alcoholic family system and the damage it does to its members. As a rule, the ACoA suffers from a lack of information about the consequences of growing up in an alcoholic family system. Often ACoAs have a general feeling that something is wrong but cannot pinpoint the source of their problem. Information groups, both large and small, usually meet for a limited period of time, and offer ACoAs basic education about the dysfunction they inherited from their parents.

The process group has a much different purpose. Its function is to provide a safe place for the ACoA to begin to feel his or her repressed feelings, and to process what it was like to grow up in an abusive family system. It is in the course of this experiencing and processing that true healing occurs. The nature of the abuse that happens in alcoholic family systems is often quite severe, and members of process groups often undergo dramatic emotional upheavals. Because of this emotional intensity process groups need to be small and intimate. The ACoA process groups that I have facilitated were limited to six people, met once a week, and lasted for two hours. These groups were open-ended, and often clients would stay for two or more years or until they felt they had completed their work.

When you, the ACoA, are looking for a therapy group to join, it is important to keep in mind that you spent a long time in an alcoholic family. Your background has affected you deeply. Any therapy that you choose will take time to be effective. A year to three years in a ongoing small group is not an unrealistic length of time to expect to stay in therapy, provided it is focused on ACoAs issues. The time in therapy will increase significantly in groups that are not focused on these issues. A former client of mine, Jennie, put it quite bluntly when she said, "For years I have gone to all kinds of groups—therapy groups, self-help groups, bonding groups, screaming groups. You name it and I've done it. It was not until I joined a group that focused on ACoAs issues that I truly believed I really began to recover from coming from an alcoholic family."

It is important to have a group facilitator who is not only skilled in leading groups but who also has a clear understanding of ACoAs issues and whose focus is on the resolution of these issues. This is critical. ACoAs issues are very much in the public eye today, and some therapists who are running ACoAs groups may actually know little

about these issues. Information about selecting a therapist
is given later on in this section.

Individual Therapy

Many ACoAs have such an overwhelming fear of groups
and of showing their feelings in a group setting that they
must start their recovery in individual sessions with a
therapist. This was the case with Earl. He was so filled
with anger, hurt, and fear that he was not appropriate for
group work. He distrusted people so much that he could
not work out emotions in group. He had tried being in an
ACoAs therapy group for a short period of time, but he
was in so much pain during group that he could not stay.
Instead, Earl worked one-on-one with a therapist until he
developed enough trust to do group work. It is important
to note here that, as in Earl's case, although individual
therapy is often extremely important to recovery, sooner
or later every ACoA must become involved in some type
of group process. To experience real recovery the ACoA
has to learn how to relate to other people in healthy ways,
and this is most effectively accomplished in a group setting. As in group therapy, the therapist must have a clear
understanding of ACoAs issues. Without an understanding
of these issues, a therapist can have a client for years and
never get to the underlying problems of ACoAs.

Family Therapy

In family therapy, two or more members of the family
go for treatment. This is an ideal situation, and with a
skilled therapist, much can be accomplished in the way of
recovery. John, a client of mine, is a good example of what
family treatment can do. His mother had gone into a
residential treatment for her ACoAs issues. After she had
been there for two weeks, John, his brother, Paul, and
their father, Harry, went to the treatment program and
stayed for two weeks. During this time the whole family
was treated, and they had the opportunity to resolve many
issues and to open healthier communication. As John put
it when he returned from the treatment program, "This

was one of the hardest things I ever did. I know that we
may never really be close as a family, but at least now we
have a chance. I really got to know my family in a way that
I thought was impossible." After watching his family's
painful struggle in treatment, John realized for the first
time they were imperfect human beings like himself. They
had fears, angers, and secrets; they felt pain, just as John
felt pain. This revelation helped John begin to deal with
his family as they were—as fellow human beings. Although working with the whole family is desirable, in
many cases this is not possible. It is important to be aware
that the ACoA can recover even though no one else in the
family seeks treatment.

Treatment Programs

There are a growing number of treatment programs that
offer help for ACoAs. Most of these are already in the
business of treating alcoholism and chemical dependency.
At first many treatment programs treated the problems of
ACoAs the same way they treated chemical dependency.
It has been heartening to see that many treatment facili-
ties, both inpatient and outpatient, now offer separate
programs for ACoAs treatment. If you decide to enter
treatment for ACoAs issues, ask the program personnel
whether they treat ACoAs issues separately from chemical-
dependency issues. If the answer is vague, or you cannot
get a straight answer, try another program. A good ACoAs
therapist can also assess whether your needs are best served
in an inpatient or outpatient setting.

In inpatient programs clients live at the facility while
receiving treatment. The treatment facility provides food
and shelter so that clients may separate from the outside
world in order to focus entirely on treatment. In most
inpatient treatment programs the time is structured and
divided between information groups, individual therapy,
and process groups. The inpatient experience can be quite
intensive, and the ACoA can make excellent progress in
beginning recovery. Inpatient treatment can last from one
to six or more weeks, depending on the program and on
the assessment of an individual's needs. It is important

that, following inpatient treatment, the ACoA continue ongoing aftercare or outpatient treatment. For most ACoAs inpatient treatment is only the start of their recovery process. Without ongoing aftercare, recovery is usually limited. Any ACoA considering inpatient treatment should inquire about the program's aftercare plan. If no outpatient aftercare is available, ACoAs need to ask for referral to a qualified therapist who can provide continuing treatment.

Outpatient aftercare is ordinarily community-based treatment where the client lives at home and attends the program in the evenings or during the day. By going to treatment for two or three hours a day the client has the opportunity to continue to work and to go home at night. There is a wide range of outpatient programs, lasting from one week to over a year. Most of the effective outpatient programs I have seen have the same components as inpatient programs: information groups, individual therapy, and process groups. As with inpatient programs, it is vital that the ACoA have the opportunity to continue long-term therapy.

One of the favorable aspects of outpatient programs is that they are generally less expensive than inpatient ones. Lastly every treatment program has advantages and disadvantages. In searching for ACoA treatment, take a look at more than one program and choose one that best suits your needs. A general rule of thumb in seeking treatment is to look for an environment in which you feel safe, and that is staffed by people who will be both honest and supportive.

Al-Anon Family Groups

The Al-Anon Family Groups consist of people who are either relatives or friends of alcoholics. Al-Anon is closely linked to Alcoholics Anonymous, and is responsible for the recovery of tens of thousands of alcoholic families. Adult children of alcoholics can find support and encouragement within this organization. In recent years there has been a tremendous increase in Al-Anon groups that focus on assisting ACoAs in the recovery process. Members of Al-Anon practice the Twelve Steps of Alcoholics Anonymous as a way to recovery, and the ACoA who works this program will add a spiritual dimension to recovery that many find is essential to healthy living. I strongly encourage my own clients—and all ACoAs—to attend ACoA-focused Al-Anon meetings on a regular basis. Because of the rapid growth of the ACoA movement, there are now ACoA Al-Anon meetings in almost every major city throughout the United States. At the back of this book is further information to help you locate the Al-Anon in your area.

National Association for Children of Alcoholics

This nonprofit organization was founded with the objective of developing a network of information and caring for young, adolescent, and adult children of alcoholics. The organization (NACoA) has grown rapidly since its inception in 1983, and now has a number of state chapters. This is a genuine grass-roots movement through which adult children can get valuable information about what is available to ACoAs in various localities. The NACoA address is listed in the resource section at the back of this book.

Summary

When an ACoA goes shopping for a therapist—and you don't have to take the first one that comes along—it is important to interview the therapist and find out what he or she knows about alcoholism and its effects on the family. This is true for group therapists, individual therapists, and therapists who work in treatment programs. If there is no qualified counselor around, then find one who is willing to learn about the issues. Give him or her this book to read and recommend some of the other books that have been written about this subject. If the therapist is not willing to learn, then find a therapist who is.

If there are no ACoA Al-Anon meetings, then find out how to go about starting one. As I stated before, many areas do not yet have the services for ACoAs, and to get treatment ACoAs will need to be creative.

Regardless of who the therapist is or what kind of treatment program is selected, it is important that treatment, to be complete and effective, include the three components described earlier. These three components are:

1. Emotional Discharge
2. Cognitive Reconstruction
3. Behavioral Action

The following sections comprise the Family Integration System. This is a system I developed over the past few years, while working with ACoAs. Although the system was designed as an adjunct to therapy, many ACoAs continue to use it after they have completed therapy so they can continue to process feelings about their family when they feel the need. Many ACoAs have successfully used the system as a prelude to therapy. Regardless of when the system has been used, it has proved itself as a therapeutic tool in the recovery process.

9
Introduction and Setup

The Family Integration System (FIS) is a systemized method designed to assist ACoAs in resolving the unfinished business that they have with their families of origin. Every untreated ACoA has fear, anger, hurt, and other painful emotions that are unresolved. Many also have difficulty in remembering their childhood. Most ACoAs do not have a sense of what it was like to be children. They have missed this magical experience, and with this loss, the sense of wonder that is part of a healthy childhood. The FIS will assist the ACoA in resolving the unresolved emotions, filling in the memory gaps and recapturing the wonder of the magical child that dwells within.

Letting go of the chains of the past and finding forgiveness for both themselves and their families is an integral part of the recovery process for ACoAs. To do this it takes many hours of work that is both painful and at times frightening. The question asked over and over by ACoAs is "Is it worth it?" The only answer can come from within. In both my personal experience and in sharing the experiences of my clients, I can, with confidence, say, "Yes, it is worth it." Those who work at their recovery do get better. The FIS has been an integral part of this recovery process for many ACoAs.

The FIS is a tool that helps the ACoA focus on the recovery process. It is an instrument that can be used at any convenient time. When a person is in therapy, he or she generally sees the therapist once or twice a week. The same is generally true for attendance at ACoA Al-Anon

groups, which most ACoAs attend once or twice a week.
This leaves a lot of free time for ACoAs to work on their
issues. In fact, most of the recovery work done by ACoAs
is done outside of the therapist's office, and the most
useful tool that I have found for this work is the FIS.

The FIS is a personal journal that is structured in a way
that will facilitate the recovery process. It is different from
a diary, or most other written records about a person's
life, in that the focus is resolving the conflict and pain that
is a direct result of growing up in an alcoholic family. It
does this by providing an arena where conflict can safely
be resolved.

Setting Up the FIS

The key to the effectiveness of the FIS is that it is
divided into sections. Each section has a purpose, and the
writer can add information, ideas, and feelings to a particular section whenever he or she feels the need. Because
entries are made in different sections of the system and at
different times, the most effective way to keep the system
is in a looseleaf book—preferably a three-ring binder. This
gives the flexibility of being able to add pages to different
sections when needed. A bound journal, with a fixed
number of pages, does not provide this option.

Selection of the looseleaf binder can be important. Select one that is both durable and pleasing to the eye. A lot
of time will be spent writing in the FIS, and purchasing a
high-quality binder in the beginning is helpful. Having an
attractive cover is helpful to some folks. A dreary, black
cover may not be as inviting to use on a regular basis as a
colorful one.

One of the many ways that the FIS is more flexible than
a diary is that it has different sections. The sections are
separated by dividers. As with the looseleaf cover, purchasing high-quality dividers in the beginning can remove
the headache of the dividers tearing loose from the binder.
Initially we will use eleven dividers. Once the FIS has
been used and the writer becomes familiar with it, he or
she is encouraged to add his or her own sections as needed.

Each divider will mark off a section. It is important that

the sections in the FIS be put into the looseleaf binder in the order given below. The sections that are used in the FIS are as follows:

1. Daily Log
2. Family Tree
3. Family Group Information Sheet
4. Family Myths
5. Personal History
6. The Magical Child
7. Family Members
8. Influential Persons
9. Affirmations
10. Spiritual Reflections
11. Integration

Now we have before us a looseleaf book—hopefully pleasing to the eye and durable—inside of which there will be eleven sections. Each section will be separated by a divider and titled. The order of the sections will be as described above. This is the basic structure for the FIS.

The information that will be put into this system is of a very personal nature. The thoughts and feelings about the family of origin, and the effects that the family have had on the person using the FIS is a very private matter. Therefore it is important to stress that anything that is written in this system is private information and need not be disclosed to anyone. The writer makes the decision as to whether this information is to be shared with anyone. This includes therapists. Most ACoAs have never really had privacy, and they have a need to establish this. The FIS is a private document that is shared only if the writer wishes.

The FIS is like a musical instrument. When it is practiced and used, the user becomes proficient. With the system the writer will enter the inner landscapes of his or her being. From these inner dimensions the hurts and pains of the past can be resolved and released; this is both painful and frightening. There is no way around this. The result, however, is the release of the chains that bind the ACoA to the past, and the freedom and joy that are the birthright of each human being.

10
The Daily Log

This, the first section of the FIS, is the chapter that i
most like a diary. Here the writer has a place to record the
day-to-day events and feelings that he or she is experienc
ing. Anything can be recorded in this section.

The daily log serves two important functions. First, i
provides a place where the writer can record the curren
events of his or her life. When this section is kept for a
long period of time, patterns of behavior that are uncon
scious can be identified and, if judged harmful, changed
Second, this section often opens up the writer to informa
tion that can be used in the other sections of the FIS
ACoAs often have vague and undefinable feelings; writing
about these feelings can bring them into focus. Then, the
ACoA can deal with the specific feeling, rather than trying
to deal with vague generalities.

Below is a typical entry in the daily log section.

> I got so angry at Jane, my wife, today. I was not only
> angry at her, but I was frustrated and angry a
> myself. It's the same thing every time. When I ge
> angry, I withdraw and don't ever say that I'm an
> gry. I just get quiet and simmer. When I try to talk, .
> choke up and don't know what to say or how to say
> I'm angry. I'm so tired of doing this. I remembe
> doing the same thing when I was a kid. Whenever
> got mad as a kid, I could not say anything about it to
> anyone. If I even showed anger, I got "the look" from
> Mom, and would just swallow the anger.

There are two important points to be made about the above entry.

First, the entry is dated. Every entry made in the FIS is to be dated. It is important for the writer to know when the entry was made, because, over a period of time, as the writer's perspective changes, the sequence of dated entries will assist the writer in seeing his or her growth.

Second, from the above entry, it is clear that the shutting down of anger is a lifelong pattern. The roots of this shutting down are in the family of origin, and specifically with the mother. Therefore an entry would also be made about the writer's mother in the family members section. There will be more specific entry techniques on how to do this later.

When starting to use the FIS, it is important to use the daily log section on a regular basis. This keeps the writer active in working in the FIS, and the writer will become more at ease in using the system. The daily log section will provide information for use in other sections. Therefore I ask people who are going to use the FIS for the first time to make an entry every day for at least thirty days. After this period of time they will be familiar with the system, and need only make entries when they feel the desire to do so.

11
The Family Tree

The family tree section of the FIS is extremely important for the ACoA. People who grow up in alcoholic families generally have a distorted sense of what their family was like, and have little information about their family history. Developing a family tree can bring a sense of clarity and order into what is generally a diffused and muddled memory.

The family tree gives an overview of the family. It is simple to do and easy to read. When done correctly, it allows the person to see his or her whole family structure on one sheet of paper. The person can see the relationships between generations, and sometimes—for the first time—is able to trace the disease of alcoholism through his or her family history.

Time and again at workshops with people who are from alcoholic families, and with individual clients who are adult children from alcoholic families, I have heard the following comments:

> *I never realized how many alcoholics I have in my family.*
>
> *I am amazed at how much I don't know about my family history.*
>
> *Seeing my family tree really highlights how alcoholism has been passed down from generation to generation.*

When developing the family tree, use your family of origin rather than the nuclear family in which you may currently be living.

The first step is to have a chart that you can use to diagram your family history. Use the following chart entitled The Family Tree as a guide, and copy it onto a larger piece of paper. Be sure to copy the chart correctly, numbers and all. This will make the instructions for filling it out easy to follow.

The horizontal lines have been numbered. As we proceed with the instruction the line that we will be working on will be identified by the corresponding number. When you are putting names on the numbered lines, use the first name, middle initial, and last name. When entering women's names on the chart, use their maiden names. This makes it much easier to trace blood lines and lineage.

Line 1. Place your own name on this line. Directly below your name, in the blank unlined space, list the name of *your* brothers and sisters.

Line 2. Place your father's name on this line. Remember to use his first name, middle initial, and last name. Directly below his name, in the blank space, list *his* brothers and sisters, that is, your uncles and aunts on your father's side.

Line 3. Place your mother's name on this line. Remember to always use the maiden name for females. Directly below your mother's name, in the blank space, list *her* brothers and sisters. That would be your uncles and aunts on your mother's side.

Line 4. Place your father's father's name (your paternal grandfather) on this line. In the spaces below list your grandfather's brothers and sisters.

Line 5. Place your father's mother's name (your paternal grandmother) on this line. In the space below her name, list your grandmother's brothers and sisters.

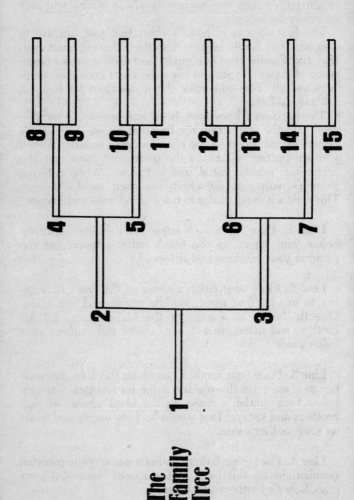

The
Family
Tree

Line 6. Place your mother's father's name (your maternal grandfather) on this line. List your maternal grandfather's brothers and sisters below his name.

Line 7. Place your mother's mother's name (your maternal grandmother) on this line. List her brothers and sisters below her name.

Lines 8 & 9. Place the names of your paternal grandfather's father (line 8) and your paternal grandfather's mother (line 9). List brothers and sisters under the appropriate name.

Lines 10 & 11. Place the names of your paternal grandmother's father (line 10) and your paternal grandmother's mother (line 11). List brothers and sisters under the appropriate name.

Lines 12 & 13. Place the names of your maternal grandfather's father (line 12), and your maternal grandfather's mother (line 13). List brothers and sisters under the appropriate name.

Lines 14 & 15. Place the names of your maternal grandmother's father (line 14) and your maternal grandmother's mother (line 15). List brothers and sisters under the appropriate name.

Do not be discouraged if there are places on your family tree that you cannot fill in. Most of us become a little hazy when we try to remember the names of our grandparents and great-grandparents. The names of their brothers and sisters are beyond most of us. It is important, however, to try to get the information that will fill in the blanks on the tree. The family tree can give us an overview of our families, and a sense that we belong to a family system.

After the family tree has been completed, review it, look at all of the names that you have filled in, and try to get a sense that each of the names represents a person—a person who was vital to your history. Remembering stories that you may have heard about different members will give you a feel for the richness of your family.

At this point place an A next to the name of any person on your chart who either is or was an alcoholic, or who may have had a drinking problem. It is important to remember that in family oral histories Great-uncle Joe will be remembered as "drinking a bit too much" rather than as an alcoholic. Next, place a C next to any family member who may have had cancer.

Coding the names in the above manner can be very enlightening. Most people who do this exercise are amazed to see, graphically displayed, that alcoholism is indeed a disease that runs in families. Although many people know this intellectually, they don't feel it emotionally until they see it in black and white, written on their family tree.

I ask people to put a C next to those family members who have had or have died from cancer, because cancer seems to be the disease of the co-dependent. I have worked with many people from alcoholic families who, when they do their family tree, find that many of their family members have either died of alcoholism or of cancer.

Feel free to make up your own code for any other diseases that you may wish to track through your family. An example could be CD for chemical dependency, or D for diabetes. Keep in mind, however, that it is the simplicity of the family tree chart that makes it effective. Try not to clutter it up too much. You may wish to make several charts and track several different items through the family history, e.g., sexual abuse or physical abuse.

The family tree is an important section of the FIS. It is from this section that we will select the people who will make up the family members section. As the system is developed you will be able to refer to this chart again and again to get important and pertinent information.

The person who grows up in an alcoholic family loses much of the memory of his or her childhood, along with a sense of belonging to a larger family system. Developing the family tree can be the first step in the process of filling in the memory loss, and becoming emotionally reintegrated into that larger system. With the awareness of his or her roots, the ACoA can use the foundations of the past to make changes in the present, so that the future will be healthier and fuller.

When you have completed as much of the family tree as you are able, proceed to the family tree questions. This is a six-question information sheet that will assist you in identifying how you felt about doing your family tree.

THE FAMILY TREE QUESTION SHEET

After completing the family tree, ask yourself the following questions, and write down the answers on a blank page. Then, insert it into the family tree section, remembering to date the entry.

1. What did I learn from this?

2. What did I relearn from this?

3. Was I surprised about anything?

4. How did I feel about filling out this sheet?

5. What meaning did this have for me?

6. Other comments and reflections

12
The Family Group Information Sheet

The family group information sheet is divided into two parts. Part one is a data collection form, and part two is a list of six questions asking how you felt about filling out the form.

The family group information sheet (part one) is much more detailed than the family tree. In the family tree you constructed a generalized overview of your family, which is extremely important for you to have. The family group information sheet, however, serves a different function. It is a detailed outline of the various subfamilies that make up your family.

The information that is compiled on the family group information sheet is important because it helps to establish the details of your history. These details will assist you in gaining a sense of belonging to your family, and also to get a sense of the individuality of each of your family members. This section in the FIS also helps you to fill in some of the memory gaps that many ACoAs have.

The following is a copy of the family group information sheet. You will need to have three blank family group sheets—one for your own nuclear family (Dad, Mom, brothers, and sisters); one for the nuclear family of your father; and one for the nuclear family of your mother. I strongly suggest that you take the time to copy the blank form below and use that copy to make additional copies as needed. You may need extra copies, particularly if you do group sheets for your great-grandparents. It will require effort on your part to write out the forms and make copies, but it is worth the effort.

As you look at the family group information sheet, you will see that it is a series of questions about your family.

The first sheet that you will fill out will be about your own family of origin. Begin by answering the first question.

> Your relationship to this family is? The correct response would be "This is my nuclear family."
> Husband—The correct answer would be your father's name.
> Birth—Your father's birthdate and his place of birth.
> Married—When and where was he married?

THE FAMILY GROUP INFORMATION SHEET
(Part One)

Your relationship to this family group: _____

HUSBAND (name): _____

Birth date: _____ Place: _____

Married date: _____ Place: _____

Death date: _____ Place: _____ Cause: _____

Major life illnesses: _____

At maturity: Ht.: _____ Wt.: _____ Hair: _____ Eyes: _____

Other marriages: _____

_____

WIFE (maiden name): _____

Birth date: _____ Place: _____

Married date: _____ Place: _____

Death date: _____ Place: _____ Cause: _____

Major life illnesses: _____

At maturity: Ht.: _____ Wt.: _____ Hair: _____ Eyes: _____

Other marriages: _____

_____

Other information: _____

_____

_____

_____

CHILDREN (in birth order):   MO. DAY YR.

                                   B. _____ Place: _____

1. _____ D. _____ Cause: _____

                                   B. _____ Place: _____

2. _____ D. _____ Cause: _____

                                   B. _____ Place: _____

3. _____ D. _____ Cause: _____

                                   B. _____ Place: _____

4. _____ D. _____ Cause: _____

                                   B. _____ Place: _____

5. _____ D. _____ Cause: _____

                                   B. _____ Place: _____

6. _____ D. _____ Cause: _____

                                   B. _____ Place: _____

7. _____ D. _____ Cause: _____

                                   B. _____ Place: _____

8. _____ D. _____ Cause: _____

                                   B. _____ Place: _____

9. _____ D. _____ Cause: _____

                                   B. _____ Place: _____

10. _____ D. _____ Cause: _____

Death—If he is dead, when and where did he die, and what was the cause?

Major life illnesses—What were the major life illnesses that he had?

At maturity—Give his height, weight, hair color, and eye color. By maturity, I mean either the way you remember him best, or the way he was described to you by others.

If you do not have any information about him, leave this blank.

Other marriages—Put any other marriages you know about.

When you complete this for your father, continue and fill out the same information for your mother (i.e., Wife—put your mother's name).

When you reach the section for other information, put

any other information that you feel is relevant to your father and mother's relationship. Be brief. An example of other information could be "Mom and Dad were married during the Depression and did not have very much money, and Dad could not find a job."

In the next section fill in—in order of birth—the children that were born to this couple (your mother and father).

B = born; fill in the month, day, and year of birth; then fill in the place of birth.
D = death; fill in the month, day, and year of death and the cause of death.

Since this is your nuclear family, your name will be among the list of children. If you were the third child born, you would be number three on the list.

You will be filling out your family group information sheets on each of the major family groups in your family tree. The next family group you will work with will be your father's family, or your paternal grandparents. Begin by answering the first question.

Your relationship to this family group is? The correct response would be "These are my paternal grandparents" (father's family).
Husband—put your grandfather's name.
Continue to complete out the rest of the blanks.
Wife—Put your paternal grandmother (father's grandmother).
Continue to answer the rest of the questions.

In the section for children your father's name would be filled in according to his birth order among his brothers and sisters, i.e., if he were the eighth born, he would be number eight.

When you complete this, fill out a group information sheet for your maternal grandmother and grandfather. Follow the steps outlined above.

If you wish, you may do information sheets for your great-grandparents. Follow the same procedures described above. You may be surprised at what you find out about your family; Colin was.

Colin, an ACoA and a recovering alcoholic, had always thought that his father's side of the family were "the drunks." It was on this side of the family that alcoholism ran rampant. His father died of it, his uncles were alcoholic, and his paternal grandfather had died of it. He had always assumed that his mother's side of the family was the nonalcoholic side. However, he had always thought it strange that his mother—who was raised in a nondrinking family and who did not drink alcohol herself—married a dyed-in-the-wool alcoholic like his father.

As Colin learned more and more about the alcoholic family and the way it behaves, he began to notice that his mother's family, although they did not drink, behaved noticeably alcoholically. When he did the family group information sheet for his maternal great-grandfather, he turned up some surprising information. He found that his grandfather was the youngest of five children, all boys. Colin also found out that all of his grandfather's brothers "drank themselves to death" and that his great-grandfather also "liked the booze." His grandfather decided at an early age that he would not drink—and never did; he had always refused to talk about his father or brothers because he was ashamed of their drinking. Colin got this information from his grandmother, who felt that, now that his grandfather was dead, it would be all right to talk about family secrets.

Finding out about the alcoholism on his mother's side of the family explained to Colin why the nondrinking side of the family behaved so dysfunctionally.

This may seem like a lot of work—and it is—but doing the family group information sheets will pay off in your having a much more in-depth understanding of your family, and of the relationship that your family members have to one another and where they fit into your personal history.

Do not be discouraged if there is a lot of information that you do not know. You can find out a great deal about your relationship to your family by what you do not know. Also some of this information will come back to you after a time. I also encourage you to talk to relatives about your family, and to do some research into your family history.

When you have filled in as much as you can of each group information sheet, answer the following questions on blank paper and insert it into the end of this section. This will complete part two of the family group information sheet.

1. What did I learn from this?

2. What did I relearn from this?

3. Was I surprised about anything?

4. How did I feel about filling out this sheet?

5. What meaning did this have for me?

6. Other comments and reflections

The family group information sheets are an integral part of the Family Integration System. It is necessary for us to dig into our past for the facts about our family history. With this information we can begin to understand what the alcoholic family system means to us and how it affects us today. With this awareness we can move forward in our individual growth process and begin to let go of the chains of unconscious behavior that bind us to the past.

13
Family Myths

This is the section in the FIS where you take the stories or tales that you have heard about your family and write them down. Up until this point in the system, you have been dealing with observable facts—facts that are concrete, like dates of birth and death, places lived, and names of relatives, both near and distant. When I use the term *myths*, I mean those stories that are passed down from one generation to another—tales that you have heard about your parents, your grandparents, or your great-grandparents. Some of the stories are true, and some are not.

There are two general types of family myths. The first is the myth of how the family perceives itself. The second type consists of those unsubstantiated stories that exist in every family that are not necessarily fact but add richness and a certain color to the family history. Alcoholic families abound with family myths. A more detailed description of the two types of family myths follows.

The first type of myth is how the family behaves, and how the family perceives itself. The basic myth of the alcoholic family is that it is normal. Alcoholic families try to hide their sometimes bizarre behavioral episodes from the world by creating the myth of being normal. This appearance of being normal is important to the family system. There is a fear of being found out, and that if found out, then someone or something will try to change the system. Some of the more common myths that most alcoholic families have are:

All families are the same as us—we are normal.

Talking about what happens in the family will just make it worse.

Someday things will get better.

We, the family, will always be there whenever you need us.

We may fight a lot, but we really stick together through thick and thin.

We always tell the truth, and hold honesty as a high value.

It's okay to lie to others outside the family; they don't understand us anyway.

These are just some of the family myths that alcoholic families have. A former client, Ann Taylor, had a family myth that was "The Taylor women are strong women and are really in control." In reality the Taylor women were sick co-dependents and untreated ACoAs. They all married alcoholics and then spent their lives trying to control them. "Strong" was substituted in this family myth for being emotionally shut down. See if you can list some of your own family myths. As you work in other sections of the FIS, you may wish to return to this section and add additional information as you remember more about your family's myths.

The other type of family myth is more akin to the legend. Every family has one or more stories in its history that takes a larger-than-life proportion. Stories such as having an ancestor who was an exiled prince or princess abound. Stories of ancestors who single-handedly won the Indian wars—or who were Indian chiefs—are some of the many myths that families have.

Do you have an Indian princess in your family history? Any pirates or other villains? How about being related to the Czar of Russia? Many family myths have a basis in fact. Over the years the facts have been embellished somewhat. This makes for good storytelling.

Myths add color and character to the family history. There is nothing wrong with them, and they are interesting to tell and to hear. At one workshop that I conducted, two people who were unrelated and did not know each other before the workshop had the same legendary figure in their family history—Daniel Boone. As they compared their family histories, it also became apparent that it would have been impossible for Daniel Boone to belong to both families; in fact, it was improbable that the legendary figure was a part of either family, but both clients grew up with this belief. Family myths can also revolve around a family character—some family member who has done eccentric things, and always seems to come out of the experience okay, if not somewhat bedraggled. You might have a Great-uncle Charlie who is remembered for "drinking a bit" and getting into trouble. One thing is certain: If your family is still talking about Great-uncle Charlie's drinking forty years later, then Great-uncle Charlie was an alcoholic.

One ACoA had a maternal grandmother who raised six children by herself during the Depression; at least two of her husbands were alcoholic. Part of her story was that in order to live rent-free, she would take jobs as a building superintendent, with the agreement that she would keep the building clean. Being of Scandinavian descent—which many people associated with cleanliness—she had no trouble finding jobs. Since she had to work at other jobs to buy food, she just never got around to cleaning the buildings, which included, during the winter, taking out the ashes from the furnaces. She would let the basement of the building fill up with ashes and then, with all her children, move to the other side of the city, taking another job as building superintendent. This story may or may not be true. It does, however, make for good telling around the dinner table at Christmastime—before the fighting starts.

Many adult children are so alienated from their families that they cannot remember any family myths. They have blocked off much of their family history because of the pain of growing up in an alcoholic system. If you are one of those who cannot remember any family myths, ask other family members what they remember.

If you cannot remember any family myths, don't be discouraged. Many ACoAs have memory loss surrounding their childhood. Also alcoholic families don't get very high scores in clear communication, and the fact is that you may not have heard any family myths. As you work through the system, some myths about your family will, in all likelihood, return to your memory. If this happens, then return to this section and write them down.

Remember that this section is about myths. The stories don't have to be factual and can, and will, be rather outlandish. Nothing is too silly for this section, so be free with your tall taletelling. Now go ahead and make some entries into this section, remembering to date the entries.

14
The Personal History Section

The personal history section of the Family Integration System is where your personal history is recorded.

Many people from alcoholic families do not have a sense of having a personal history. The memories of their past experiences are often sketchy and unclear. One of the main reasons for this is that many times the memories of childhood are so painful, they are repressed.

The purpose of this section is to assist the adult child in filling in the lost memories of his or her childhood, and resolving the emotional trauma that often accompanies these forgotten memories. When these memory gaps are filled in, the person has the opportunity to process the feelings that were repressed, along with the actual memories. It is important that these memories and feelings be processed. Even though a person may not have the memory of an event that was traumatic, the physical and psychological effects of the event often still have an effect on that person. *Unless emotions attached to that trauma are resolved, the person will be affected for the rest of his or her life.*

One of the purposes of the Family Integration System is to assist the adult child in processing those lost memories and feelings. It is with the processing of these feelings that behavior changes, and old patterns of thoughts and feelings are transformed into healthier ways of dealing with other people and living in the world.

In the personal history section we will be using proved techniques to assist the ACoA in the process of resolving and letting go. The first time that you use the system, follow the directions and work at your own pace. As you use this section, and the other sections, more and more information about your life will become known to you. This is why the system uses a looseleaf-book format, so that as you learn more about yourself, you will be able to add this information to the different sections of your journal. Remember that when making an entry into the Family Integration System, date it. This is important. As you add information to the system the date will assist you in tracking your insights and progress.

The first technique that will be discussed for use in the personal history section is dialoguing with the physical body.

One of the most effective ways to fill in the memory gaps, both emotional—not feeling anything about an event—and not remembering the event itself, is to dialogue with your own physical body. Our physical bodies contain a wisdom about the events of our lives that is generally untapped. Our bodies have been with us the entire time of our lives, and by using a writing technique called dialoguing, a vast wealth of personal information—not just the factual information, but also the reexperiencing of repressed emotions and memories—can be obtained.

There are four major steps in setting up a dialogue:

1. Meditation
2. Writing a focusing statement
3. Writing milestones
4. Dialoguing

Each of these steps will be explained in detail.

Meditation

The first step in the process is to set the correct frame of mind. This is why the process is begun with a simple meditation. By becoming quiet and getting centered, the process of dialoguing will proceed more smoothly and easily. Begin the meditation by finding a comfortable position and taking two or three deep, easy breaths. The next step is to focus your awareness on the process of breathing. Allow your attention to remain focused on the process of breathing for two or three minutes. Remember, it is normal to forget that you are trying to focus on your breath, and to focus on other things. When this occurs, remind yourself that your intention is to focus on your breath, and refocus on that process. Simple, isn't it? Pause right now and take a few minutes to try out this meditation technique.

Focusing Statement

The second step in the dialoguing process is to write down a focusing statement about what kind of relationship you have with your physical body. This focusing statement need be no longer than a paragraph in length, but must contain how you feel about your body. Consider these questions: Do I think that I am too fat or too thin? Am I too short or too tall? Do I just ignore my physical body until something goes wrong with it or do I constantly obsess over it? The focusing statement states what kind of present *relationship* you have with your body. Below is an example of a focusing statement.

> *I really feel out of touch with my body. I have not taken very good care of it, and most of the time I don't notice it unless it gets sick or hurt. I really feel that my body has betrayed me at times, but I am also looking forward to getting to know my body better.*

It is important to write the focusing statement as if you were talking bout another person.

Milestones

The third step in the dialoguing process is to list your life milestones. Life milestones are the major events that have happened in your life. These events can be either physical or emotional in nature. The milestones are the markers on the road of your life. They represent those events that have helped to shape who you are and how you view the world.

As a person grows old and changes, the milestones that are important will also change. Therefore, it is important to redo your milestones each time you dialogue with your body. Writing down the milestones also helps to set the mood for being open to the dialogue process.

When you are making your milestone list, it is important to keep the number of milestones to a manageable length, and to group the milestones into ten-year intervals. Try to limit the number of milestones in each ten-year interval to five or six. Therefore, the number of milestones will vary according to your age. The milestone list is an overview of a person's life, not a detailed account of every event. Thus, the list is fairly short. Many ACoAs try to forget that the first ten to fifteen years of their lives ever happened. That is why it is important to group the milestones in ten-year intervals: It forces the writer to do milestones for the first ten years of life. The following are the milestones of Jane, an ACoA.

Major Life Milestones

0 to 10 years old
being born
playing doctor with friends
being beaten
having tonsils out
Mom and Dad fighting, getting divorced
being sexually molested by step-dad

11 to 20 years old
discovering sex
using drugs and alcohol
hating being tall
being awkward around boys
pimples
getting married

20 to 30 years old
birth of my son, Richard
death of father from alcoholism

getting divorced
feeling alone and isolated
auto accident with broken legs
getting sober

The above milestones contain both emotional and physical life experiences, and stop during the 20 to 30 age grouping. This is because Jane was in her late twenties when she did this list. When doing your own milestones, stop at your current age.

Dialoguing

Dialoguing is the next step. The process of doing a written dialogue is very much like writing a script for a play. The difference here is that the dialogue will be between you and your physical body. Now, this may sound strange to you, but give it a chance. As I said before, this is one of the most powerful sections in the FIS, and the dialoguing technique will be used in other sections. Most people, when they start out dialoguing, feel a little awkward and unsure of what they are doing. That's okay; the more times you dialogue, the easier and more spontaneous it will become.

Below is an example of dialoguing with the body by Jane, the woman whose focusing statement and milestones were used in the above examples.

Jane: This seems silly to me.
Body: I know.
Jane: Am I really talking to my body?
Body: Yes, you are.
Jane: I have never talked to you before.
Body: I know. You never listen to me either.
Jane: What do you mean by that?
Body: Well, you just ignore me when I am trying to tell you something.
Jane: I do?
Body: You do? Ha! What about when you get out of breath when you are going up a flight of stairs? I'm telling you that you need to exercise me more. And

> *when your neck and shoulders hurt, I'm telling you
> that you are tense. You don't listen, you ignore.*
> **Jane:** *Well, if you put it that way, maybe I do. I'll try
> to pay more attention to what you are trying to tell
> me.*
> **Body:** *Good.*
> **Jane:** *Good-bye for now.*
> **Body:** *Good-bye. Stay in touch.*

As can be seen in the above example, dialoguing can
bring about some surprising results. The more you dialogue, the easier it becomes, and the more surprising the
information that is disclosed will be. When you are doing
a dialogue with your body, you can ask it specific questions about events that have happened in your life, and
how you felt about those events. These events can range
from how and what you experienced when being abused
as a child, to the joy of a dimly remembered happy event.

When dialoguing, feelings and emotions that have been
repressed for years are often processed. This can be painful. It is, however, worthwhile. With the processing of
these repressed feelings, the pain of the experience can be
released, and the writer will be set free of the event.

The above technique of dialoguing is very effective for
exploring personal history, and this method will be used
extensively later in the FIS. Another way to fill in personal history effectively is by using the milestones as entry
points into the past. Milestones are events or happenings
that are full of emotional charges. The milestone is like the
tip of the iceberg; it is an expression of much more than it
appears to be. Like the iceberg, when the milestone is
examined in depth, there is an enormous amount of information and "frozen" emotions that reside beneath the
surface.

This hidden psychic material that each of us has within
can be released by a very simple but powerful writing
technique. The first step is, of course, to have a milestone
list. We shall use Jane's milestones, listed on pp. 113–114,
to illustrate the technique.

Jane, like many ACoAs, had large periods of time during her childhood that she did not remember. One of

those periods was the time when her mother and father got their divorce. She remembered the time only vaguely and attached no importance to the divorce. To her it was "no big deal." To fill in some of the blank periods of time surrounding the divorce, Jane used the following technique.

First, she picked the milestone to work with (in this case, "Mom and Dad fighting, getting divorced"). Second, she got a clean sheet of paper, dated it, and wrote the milestone at the top of her paper. Third, having decided to use this milestone, Jane thought about what she knew about this period of her life. She asked herself these questions and wrote them down at the top of her paper:

1. Where was I living at this time in my life?
2. Whom was I living with at this time in my life?
3. What was important to me at this time in my life?
4. What was I afraid of at this time in my life?
5. Who were my friends at this time in my life?

Jane then began to write about the milestone. To begin the writing process she started by using the phrase *This was a time in my life when* . . . and allowing the writing to flow. When the writing begins, it is very similar to following a single thread through a spool; it leads through a maze of different and surprising places. When a person writes using this method, each thought triggers new thoughts and memories that have been forgotten or repressed. With the remembering also comes the experiencing of the emotional charge that was repressed at the time the event was repressed or forgotten. With the remembering also comes the release and the letting go of the pain. Below is an excerpt from Jane's writing.

> *This was a time in my life when Mom and Dad were fighting—getting divorced. I don't remember much about this time in my life, but I do remember being scared all of the time. Mom and Dad yelled and screamed a lot. I remember hiding under the kitchen table one night, and Dad hit Mom and knocked her down. He had a knife and was drunk. I was so scared, I couldn't even cry. I thought that if I moved,*

he would see me and kill me too. I thought he was killing her, and all I could do was hide and watch. I was so afraid. She was all full of blood from where he hit her on the face, and she was crying. He left, and I went to bed. They always fought over me, and I still don't know what I did to make them fight like that.

As Jane continued to write, more and more of the repressed memories surfaced, and she could see just how afraid she really was, and why she "forgot" what was happening in her life during that period of time. With the memories often comes the releasing of repressed emotions. It is important to realize that, even though Jane had forgotten much about this period of time in her life, what happened during that period still affected her. The fear, anger, and hurt that she repressed then affected her present relationships.

This is a powerful technique, and each of the personal milestones contain much information that cries out for release. Use it for all of your milestones. The results may, in the short term, be painful, but in the long term there will be release from repressed emotions and painful memories. The following is an outline of how to use this process.

1. Get a clean sheet of paper and date it.
2. Select the milestone that you wish to write about, and write it at the top of the paper.
3. Write down the five questions:
   a. Where was I living at this time in my life?
   b. Whom was I living with at this time in my life?
   c. What was important to me at this time in my life?
   d. What was I afraid of at this time in my life?
   e. Who were my friends at this time in my life?
4. Reflect for a moment on the milestone and the questions.
5. Begin to write, starting with the phrase *This was a time in my life when* . . .

The following is a list of memory-jogging questions that I have found useful in assisting ACoAs in filling in the blank periods that most have in their past. Add this list of questions, with the answers, to this section of the FIS.

Were you wanted at birth?
Were you afraid of the dark?
How were you punished as a child?
Were you left alone a lot?
Were you beaten? How often?
Where did you go to hide as a child?
How did you feel when your parents argued?
Were you threatened with physical violence?
Do you think you were sexually abused (intercourse, fondled, watched) as a child?
Do you remember being held and nurtured?
When did you discover your sexuality?
Did you engaged in sex play as a child? Were you caught? Punished?
Was there a divorce? More than one?
How old were you when you first remember a parent drunk?
How did you feel when a parent was drunk?
Did you ever see a parent nude and drunk? How did you feel?
Did you have friends over to your house?
Did a family member die? How?
When did you begin to masturbate? Were you caught?
Did you like school?
How many friends did you have?
Did you have any childhood homosexual experiences?
Did you ever see one parent hit another? How often?
Did your parents ever threaten each other or fight with weapons such as guns or knives?
Did you feel trapped?
How old were you when you first had intercourse? How did you feel about it?
Were you able to show anger?
Did you cry? How do you show anger and hurt today as an adult?
What questions and answers would you add to this list?

The personal history section is an integral part of the Family Integration System. It is a section that is never really completed, but is continually added to and reviewed. Through the growing awareness and memory of your personal history and the filling in of the emotional and mental blank spots, a continuity with yourself and your past can be established. When this occurs, recovery from the painful and confusing programmed patterns of feelings and behaviors that ACoAs unconsciously carry around with them can—and does—happen.

15
The Magical Child

In this section of the FIS the focus will be on the ACoA getting in touch with his or her magical child. The magical child is that part of the ACoA that is pure and innocent; the child that was untouched by the external experience of growing up in an alcoholic family. No matter how terrible the experience—from repeated sexual abuse and beatings to the cold icy family that never touched each other in kindness or affection—there is a part of the human psyche that remains untouched. This untouched part of the psyche is full of the unconditional love that only a child can have. It is this part that is the magical child.

This child within, this magical child, longs to be released—released so that he or she can love, play, and enjoy the spontaneous experiences of life. Every person has a magical child who lives within, deep down somewhere near his or her heart. The ACoA is no exception. The ACoA, however, has been forced to bury that magical child deeper than most other people. The environment of the alcoholic family does not lend itself to having a fun-filled, loving childhood. A child in an alcoholic family must learn to survive and to protect him- or herself. This is a full-time job, and most ACoAs have a sense of having never been a child, or of having lost their childhood.

The process of getting in touch with the magical child is simple. The child is longing for release. All it needs is encouragement and a pathway to express itself. Although the methods of releasing this child are simple, for most ACoAs it is not an easy task. They have, for the most part, had years of practice repressing this child because it was not safe to allow the child to be expressed. This child must be expressed, and one of the primary pathways is by expression through the injured child.

Every ACoA also has an injured child who lives within. This injured child is the child who lived through the disaster of the alcoholic family and was not allowed to express his or her hurt, loss, anger, rage, guilt, fear, and shame. This injured child must find expression; it must be allowed to release the pent-up emotions that have been repressed for years. It must be allowed to cry and to rage. Paradoxically it is through the expression of the pain and fear of the injured child that the joy and love of the magical child can be experienced.

The healing of the injured child releases the magical child. This healing process is on the one hand painful and on the other hand touching and joyful. The injured child needs the nurturing and love that he or she was denied. As the child within is healed the adult is also healed; as the child within is loved and nurtured the child within loves unconditionally and nurtures the adult. As the injured child is healed a transformation takes place: The injured is transformed into the magical, and in the world of magic anything can happen. The adult becomes healed and acquires those magical qualities of self-acceptance and love, of spontaneity and laughter.

The process begins by the ACoA becoming aware of the child within and then getting in contact with that child. To do this requires some preparation and work. Although many ACoAs have few memories of their childhood, that is not a barrier to getting in touch with the inner child. Everyone can contact his or her inner child, regardless of memory loss.

One of the most effective ways of contacting this child is by writing a letter to him or her. The experience of writing a letter to the child within is often powerful. In order to set a conducive atmosphere for the letter writing, get a photograph of yourself as a young child and carry it around for approximately one week. Every so often, take out the photo and look at it. Imagine what was going on in your life at the time the photograph was taken. While doing this, see if it is possible to get any baby books about yourself, and collect any other pictures of yourself as a child that you may have, and put them into a photograph album. If you have any childhood toys, get them and play with them (or at least think about playing with them).

As you are doing the above go back to the personal history section and look at your early-childhood milestones. Write about these milestones, using the writing techniques described in the personal history section. If you don't have any photographs of yourself at a young age, don't despair. Just writing about your early-childhood milestones is enough to set the stage for you to contact your magical child.

After you have done the preparation, find some time alone and sit down with your pictures and your written milestones and take a few minutes to reflect upon your childhood. Look at the pictures and read your milestones. Then take a blank piece of paper, date it, and write a letter to your inner child.

Below is a letter an ACoA wrote to his injured child.

Dear injured child,

I love you, my little friend. No one meant to hurt you so deeply and keep you from feeling love. I want to comfort you and take care of you. I will not abandon you because you are dearly loved. Please help me to hear you and to listen to what you are saying. We can work together toward finding God within, so that we don't have to be injured again.

It is okay to talk to me about how you feel. All the anger, jealousy, hurt feelings, envy, possessiveness, and fear do not have to be hidden anymore. It is human to feel those feelings, and then move on to feel other feelings. You don't have to hide them anymore. And you don't have to trade off by trying to be something you are not. You can just be yourself and feel good about it. It is okay to be alive and it is okay to need to learn how to talk about how you feel, and to learn how to forgive. We can learn to trust each other by spending time together and learning to listen.

I want also to apologize to you for not trying to listen harder. I want also to apologize for not knowing how to take care of you and always looking outside of us to find the answers. We can learn how to help and love each other if we have patience. Goodbye for now.

I love you,
Lee

Continuing to write letters and keeping the inner child in your consciousness is a process that is very healing. In the above letter a pathway for healing was opened up by Lee, the adult who wrote the letter. As this healing pathway is opened wider and wider, the child within becomes freer and freer. With this freedom comes more and more healing. The next step in this healing process is creating a means for the child to communicate with the adult. This can also be done very effectively by letter writing.

In setting the atmosphere for the magical child to respond, there are several guidelines that are very useful to follow.

1. Become quiet for a few minutes.
2. Reflect on your childhood, using a picture of yourself or your milestones.
3. Write a letter to the magical child and ask for a return letter.
4. Write a letter from the magical child to the adult. When writing this letter, write with the hand that you do *not* normally write with. For instance, if you write with your right hand, then use your left hand when the child is responding.

Step 4 may feel difficult and awkward, but it is very effective in allowing the magical child to express him- or herself. On the following page is a letter to the magical child by an ACoA named Susie and a response from Little Susie.

Dear Little Susie,

I want you to know I am very fond of you even
though I don't know you very well yet. I'd like to get
to know you and maybe learn from you too. Sometimes I feel you are hiding.

Let me introduce myself. I am a big kid and I have
a job. I work in a tall building, and I have a big
picture window. Sometimes there are rainbows I think
you would enjoy. Do you like rainbows? What is it
you like about them? Please tell me.

Sometimes I'm very frightened because of what happened to you, and I get afraid it will happen to me
too. To tell the truth, I'm afraid all the time. Do you
get afraid? What are you afraid of? What do you do
about it? I need help with this.

I think we could work together and play together if
we knew each other better. I have some very nice
friends I would like you to meet.

Please write back and tell me what you would like
to do, the most. What do you think we could really
have fun doing? I don't really know about fun or
about playing, but I know you do.

> With my love and best wishes,
> Susie

Dear Susie,
I got your letter and
it was nice, I am glad
you want to be friends,
I really do and don't
be afraid because
God loves us all. We can
play together anytime
my mom says yes and
that's you. Love, Susie

As you can see from Susie's letters, the result of using this letter-writing technique can be both surprising and healing. Notice in the letter from Little Susie to the adult Susie not only that the penmanship looks childlike but also the way the letter is written. The letter, if read aloud, sounds as if a child had written it—which is, of course, true.

After the opening up of the communication between Susie the adult and Susie the child, a tremendous amount of healing took place. Susie became much more playful and humorous; life had a lot more laughter than before. As a matter of fact, Susie had a hard time taking anything seriously for quite some time. She would just bubble over with laughter.

Another effective way to open up communication with the magical child is through dialoguing. Dialoguing with the child is very similar to dialoguing with the body. The same technique is used, but the focus is different. When we are dialoguing with the magical child, information and feelings often occur that are quite unexpected. Below is the way to set up the dialoguing process.

1. Meditation: Take a few deep breaths and relax.
2. Focusing statement: Write a statement that reflects the relationship that you currently have with your magical child.
3. Milestones: List the milestones of your magical child's life.
4. Dialoguing: Write a dialogue with your magical child as if you were writing a script.

Although I feel that it is important to follow all of the above steps, many times the people to whom I teach these techniques take shortcuts. After they have used the system enough and have a feel for it, they sometimes leave off steps in the process. Although I don't encourage this, I have found that people who use this system creatively often come up with ideas that really work for them. Below is a dialogue between an ACoA named Steve and his ten-year-old self. You will notice that the milestones are missing.

Steve at 10 years old.

As I consider you, I'm aware that you may have information or feelings that you would like to share.

Steve: *Hello, Little Steve.*

Little Steve: *Hello.*

Steve: *You were so sad in the dream I had. Would you like to tell me about it?*

Little Steve: *I'm real sad that Dad is gone. I really counted on him to be there. We had some good times together, but those days are all gone.*

Steve: *Did you really expect him to always be there?*

Little Steve: *Yeah. It could have gotten better as more time passed.*

Steve: *So what happened?*

Little Steve: *He got weird. I remember being afraid of him and being afraid of visiting him.*

Steve: *It's confusing, because my memories are of the fear and confusion, and my dreams are sad.*

Little Steve: *I wish I could feel sad.*

Steve: *Maybe you need to get mad first. He left me.*

Little Steve: *When?*

Steve: *When he left the house after the divorce, dummy.*

Little Steve: *But he came back to get you.*

Steve: *He came back for Greg [brother].*

Little Steve: *Who did you really want to go with?*

Steve: *You sound like a damn adult. Why does everybody figure it has to be one way or the other?*

Little Steve: *I just wanted it to be okay. I didn't want to make a decision. I'm afraid I made the wrong one. I couldn't tell Mom "No, I don't want to stay with you." I always had to tell her what she wanted to hear. Always.*

Steve: *But you say the same things about Dad.*

Little Steve: *Now you get the idea. I'm stuck. I'd like to tell them both to quit bothering me about this stuff. Why don't you?*

Steve: *I think I will. Thanks for talking to me, Little Steve. Bye for now.*

Little Steve: *Okay. Bye-bye.*

From the above dialogue Steve was able to tell his parents to quit bothering him and to stop forcing him to make choices that he did not want to make. He was also able to release the guilt that he had about staying with his mother and not going with his father. It became clear that he was guiltless at ten years old, and that things were not either-or but that there were many different choices that could be made without feeling guilty.

From the magical child much information can be learned and many repressed feelings can be released. Using this section of the FIS can be a wonderful, freeing experience. I encourage you to be creative with this section. If you release your magical child, your creativity will know no bounds, and you will be able to use these procedures in ways that will both benefit and amaze you.

16
Family Members

The family members section of the FIS is where the ACoA will have the opportunity to explore the relationships that he or she has with each family member. This section is divided into subsections, one for each of the members in the family. Every person who appears on the family tree should have a subsection in this chapter. Even those family members whom you do not personally know or whom you think have had no impact on your life need to have a place in this section.

The ACoA is full of unresolved conflict as a result of being raised in an alcoholic family. The alcoholic family system prevents its members from resolving conflict and working through painful emotional states. All ACoAs have unresolved issues with their family members. It is the resolving of these issues that is one of the keys to the recovery process for ACoAs. The ACoA is full of repressed fear, anger, hurt, rage, guilt, shame, and other painful emotional states that are a direct result of the way various family members treated him or her.

This section is a place where the ACoA can examine and resolve these issues. In many cases, this is the only safe place for the ACoA to work out painful issues with family members. Remember that one of the rules is the rule of silence, which inhibits the ACoA from talking to family members about painful issues. Many adult children are so full of fear and feel so inadequate that they are afraid to try to talk to a parent or another family member. This section is a safe place where the ACoA can express feelings about any member of the family.

There are several other reasons why this section is so important. Family members are very often reluctant—or downright unwilling—to talk about the issues that the ACoA wishes to talk about. Even though the ACoA may be ready to deal with what happened in the family, other family members may never be willing or ready to do this. For this reason it is important for the ACoA to have a medium where he or she, without the family member being involved, can work on the painful issues of being raised in an alcoholic family. This section is ideal for this. The ACoA can, in his or her own time and at whatever depth he or she wishes, deal with and resolve issues with other family members that are inhibiting emotional and spiritual growth.

Many alcoholics and co-dependents die premature deaths. These deaths vary from violent accidents to slow, drawn-out alcoholic deaths. Whatever the reason, death may end a life, but it does not end a relationship. ACoAs often feel frustrated in their quest for recovery; because an important person in their lives has died, they feel that they will never get any resolution with that person. This is not true. Many ACoAs with whom I have worked have processed their anger and hurt at parents, or other important family members who have died. Once ACoAs overcome the guilt of having negative feelings about a person who has died, they often move quite rapidly through the anger and hurt that have been repressed for years. This leads the ACoA into a state of forgiveness and peace with the person in question.

Many ACoAs have mixed feelings about using this section. One of the more common responses that I have heard from ACoAs about this is "Why should I use this to communicate with family members when I can talk to them face to face?" This face-to-face communication generally does not happen. The ACoA is also using either-or thinking. Either they have to talk face to face or not at all. Most ACoAs opt for not at all, saying that someday they will talk things out. And because of putting it off, they never do.

Another response that is common is "if they [the family members] don't want to talk to me, then I am not going to try to talk to them." Remember, what is happening in this section is that the ACoA is healing him- or herself. Any method that helps in this process is an important tool for the ACoA to use. It really does not matter what is going on in the family. The ACoA can be healed and recover. And this is a powerful section in which this process can occur.

There are two primary techniques used in the family members chapter. The first technique that will be examined is dialoguing. The second technique is letter writing. Both of these techniques will be familiar to you from previous sections. Basically the techniques do not change from one section to another; only the application of the techniques changes. Dialoguing and letter writing may be used for many different purposes, and here they will be used to assist the ACoA in resolving conflict with individual family members.

As in dialoguing with the body, when dialoguing with a family member, the same form is followed, but the purpose is different. When the ACoA dialogues with a family member, it is to bring to light feelings about that family member that were repressed during childhood. Not only does the process reactivate repressed feelings, but often also reactivates memories of actual events that were "forgotten" because they were too painful to remember.

There is a very concrete reason for reactivating these childhood memories. Unless the repressed emotions can find a release, they will not be processed. Without the release the ACoA will not be able to get free of the emotional chains that bind him or her to the alcoholic family. Where there is no release, there is no freedom. Ultimately freedom allows the ACoA to make choices about how to live a happy, joyful existence. Working in the family members section is a way for the ACoA to find this release and freedom.

As was stated before, the way the dialogue is set up is similar in form to the previous dialogue with the body. The key to successful dialoguing is to become spontaneous. This may take a certain amount of practice. Following the outlined steps will help to set the atmosphere for deep, spontaneous interaction. The following are the basic steps to use when setting up a dialogue with a family member.

1. Meditation
2. Focusing statement
3. Milestones
4. Dialoguing

Each of these steps will now be described in detail.

Meditation

The first step in the process is to set the correct frame of mind. This is why the dialoguing process is begun with a simple meditation. By becoming quiet and centered, the dialoguing will flow much more smoothly and freely. Begin the meditation by taking two or three deep, easy breaths. Then focus your awareness on the process of breathing. Be aware of your breath as it flows in and out of your body. Allow your attention to remain focused on your breathing process for two or three minutes. Remember, it is normal to forget that you are trying to focus on your breathing and to allow your thoughts to wander. When you find yourself doing this, gently refocus your attention on breathing. This is a simple but effective method of becoming quiet and centered. If you find another method that works for you, feel free to use it; but whatever method of meditation you use, please do not skip this step.

Focusing Statement

The focusing statement is a statement about what kind of a relationship you have with the person with whom you are going to dialogue. It is a short paragraph that states who this person is, how you currently feel about him or her, and what the current status of your relationship is. The focusing statement is stated in the now. This is important: The statement is about how your relationship is at the time that you are going to write the dialogue.

Below is a focusing statement for the family members section of the FIS of an ACoA named Tom. I will use Tom's writing as an example of not only the focusing statement, but also for the milestones and the actual dialoguing. This will keep the examples consistent.

> *You are my father, and as I consider your life and our relationship I feel angry. You are dead, and when I think of you, I get mad, and feel guilty for being mad. I don't want to be angry at you, but I am, and I don't know what to do with it. I feel that after what you did to me, I have a right to be angry.*

Tom's focusing statement sets the tone for how he is currently feeling about his relationship with his father. As Tom continues to work on the issues with his father his feelings will change. That's why it is important to write a new focusing statement each time you are going to dialogue.

Milestones

In dialoguing with family members—or anyone else— always write the milestones of the person you are going to dialogue with, as if the person were writing his or her own milestones. This is important. Use their voice and begin each milestone with *I* or *My*.

You can only use the information about the person that you know. Don't worry about not having enough information; just use what you have available. When you dialogue, you will access information that you did not know was available to you. The milestones are important because they get you in touch with the other person's point of view and help to set the stage for the dialoguing process. As issues are resolved the milestones will change.

In order to keep the list to a length that is useful, limit the number of milestones to ten or twelve. Any more than this is generally unmanageable, and any less is generally too sketchy. When working with someone whom you know very little about, or maybe a great-great-grandmother, you may not be able to come up with ten or twelve milestones. That's okay; work with what you have. As you dialogue, you may find out that you know more than you realized, and in future dialogues you will be able to add more milestones.

Here is a milestone list for Tom's father.

I was born in 1908.

I was sent to military school.

I fought with my brother, Jack.

I went to work with my father.

My brother killed himself.

I got married and had two sons.

My wife and I got a divorce.

My son Jay killed himself.

I moved to Dallas.

My son Tom went to prison.

I was abused as a child.

I died in June 1983.

When developing a milestone list for a family member, it is not necessary to put the milestones in chronological order. Write them down as you think of them.

Dialoguing

Dialoguing is like writing a script between two people. Imagine what a script between two people would look like. First one person would talk, and then the other person would talk. As the script progressed, the dialogue would continue to flow between the two people who are talking to each other. This is what happens when you are dialoguing. A conversation takes place between you and the family member with whom you are dialoguing. Like a good conversation, the dialogue process is an exchange of information, feelings, and ideas.

The first time that dialoguing is attempted, it may feel

strange; it may even feel contrived. Don't worry about this, and at this point don't quit. As you continue to dialogue and become familiar with doing it, the process will become easier and easier. As the dialoguing process continues it will become more and more spontaneous. With this increasing spontaneity, you will find that the dialogue will begin to write itself, and you will be amazed at the way it turns out. The conversation will travel in directions that you would never have dreamed of. You will have access to information that you did not previously have. You will be able to express painful emotions such as anger and hurt, and receive a response. With the expression of these emotions release can occur, and with release, forgiveness. The following is a dialogue between Tom (the same person whose focusing statement and milestones we have been using) and his father.

> **Tom:** *Well, Dad, as I consider your milestones, I see that I was not the only one to lose a brother to suicide. We have had a lot of similar experiences.*
>
> **Dad:** *Yes, we have. I've been angry most of my life too.*
>
> **Tom:** *I'm so goddamn sick of playing the games I learned from you. You always used to get me in a double bind. I was damned if I did and damned if I didn't. I felt like I had to act just so, or else I had failed. I'm tired of feeling like a failure.*
>
> **Dad:** *Well, then, I guess it's time to change. You're on your own now, boy.*
>
> **Tom:** *Well, thanks a lot! Just when I needed you, just when I started to think for myself, you got scared and freaked out, and left it all behind you.*
>
> **Dad:** *I was hurting too much. All my dreams were falling apart. You were the last person I wanted to hurt.*
>
> **Tom:** *I saw how weak you were then, and I was scared and alone when you left. I really needed someone in my life, someone to be there for me, and I'm still pissed off that you were not there for me.*

Dad: It seemed to me that you were taking sides with your mother, that you did not want me to be there.

Tom: Me want! I was just a kid. I didn't know what I wanted. I know that I needed you, and that you disappeared.

Dad: All my life I felt that I was leaving, bailing out of something. But, damn it, I didn't know any other way. That was the only way I knew how to deal with things.

Tom: I have been doing that for most of my life too. But now I am stopping that kind of behavior.

Dad: In the final analysis I suppose none of us had the strength or the willingness to stay. In one way or another we all found a way to leave.

Tom: Thanks for talking to me, Dad. I'm sorry about Uncle Cliff. I love you.

Dad: I love you too, Son, and Son, you are on your own now, but you are not alone. God bless you.

Dialoguing can be a powerful tool in the recovery process. Through this process, we can access the previously inaccessible and reach the unreachable. The above example of a focusing statement, milestones, and dialoguing is an actual section taken from an adult child's FIS, and I believe it points out some of the power that this process contains.

Letters

Writing letters to family members is another powerful method of both reestablishing communications and releasing emotions. As was stated before, many ACoAs are unable or unwilling to communicate with family members. This happens for a variety of reasons: death, distance, fear, or an unwilling family member. Whatever the reason, writing a letter that remains unmailed is a way for the ACoA to vent emotions. It is also a way to say things to a particular family member that would otherwise not be said.

An important aspect to the letter-writing technique is

that the letter that is written is not mailed and is for the writer's eyes only. As with all of the other writings in the FIS, this absolute privacy gives the writer freedom to write whatever he or she feels without having to explain or defend what was written. This freedom often allows the ACoA to tap into feelings that were not allowed to be felt during childhood. Anger, rage, hurt, grief, and a multitude of other feelings that were repressed are very often experienced and released during letter writing.

Some alcoholic families do not allow their children to show anger. Other families have a taboo on displaying grief. Some families allow no emotions to show at all. Each family is different, and each child in the family responds differently. Letter writing is an effective and safe way for the ACoA to begin to feel the taboo emotions that he or she has repressed against particular family members.

Letter writing is simple. All you need to do is get a blank piece of paper, date it, and begin to write as if you were writing a letter. As you are writing, allow yourself to write down all those things that you would like to say but were not able to. For example, you may already know that you are angry at a parent, but you may be unable to tell that parent. Then go ahead and write an anger letter. Or it could be that a brother, or sister, has hurt you, and you are unable to speak to him or her about it. Write a hurt letter to that person.

Below is a copy of a letter that an ACoA named Kattie wrote to her deceased alcoholic father.

> *Dear Daddy,*
>
> *I have to write you now, because if I don't, I think I will keep going crazy. I've been afraid to write you, because I'm afraid of you and always have been.*
>
> *You know I have always tried to be perfect for you, to make you happy so that you could never be angry with me again. The time you were so mad at me when I was around six made me decide this. I told the boy next door that I would pull off his penis if he pulled my hair again. Right then you jerked me up and dragged me in the house. First you took me in and put me in my bed and told me to "just think abou'*

what I had said" and said you would be back. It was a horrible, short interval: I felt as if I had done the worst thing possible in the world. You came back, stood me up, and stripped me naked; then you whipped off your belt—I still remember the whistle it made when it cleared the loops—then you begin to beat me across the back of my thighs and my bottom until I had huge welts and bruises the width of the belt strap. I was ashamed to wear shorts or go swimming for weeks after that because of the bruises—I didn't want to have to explain. There were other beatings, other humiliations, that I remember, but this was the first one. Why did you do this to me?

I also remember other times, times when I sat in your lap, in the big leather chair. I felt so secure, so loved by you. Remember the time on the boat, when you held me and let me steer? It was wonderful.

Daddy, it's so hard for me to write you now because I'm so afraid. All my life you gave me reasons to be frightened of you, and then you were the only one who could quell the fear—no one else would do. Well, I need to tell you about all those fears you left me with when you died—the fear of men, of sex, of my own self-worth, of doing things on my own and for myself.

I am so angry with you. I was so angry, so furious, so frustrated, and so obsessed with you my entire life. Please let me go.

Daddy, I am so tired of being your little girl. I was so little. Why did you hurt me? I loved you so. And I know you loved me. That's what I don't understand. You became so ugly and pushed me away. You were so sick. . . .

I've never been able to talk to you before. I've never been able to tell you how I feel. This is good, but I can't write anymore. Good-bye for now.

Love,
Kattie

As can be seen from this example, letter writing can be a powerful technique to help unlock memories and feelings, and to express what has not been expressed. I encourage you to experiment with letter writing. Try different things. For instance, if you are going to write an anger letter to a family member, try using a red pen. The color red seems to make writing about anger easier. Be creative.

The section for family members can be used for more than dialoguing and letter writing. Since you will have a subsection for each family member, you can also make minientries about how you are feeling about a particular family member. Or you can write an entry about an interaction with a family member and tell how you felt about what happened between the two of you. This keeps all pertinent information and interaction about a family member in one location. Then when you wish to look at how much work you have done with any particular member, you will be able to go to their subsection and see.

An example of a short entry in Mother's subsection follows.

> *I talked to Mother on the phone today. She tried to do the same old thing. She wanted me to relay information to my sister without doing it herself. She always does things like this. This time I said no, I told her to call Judy herself. She didn't sound too happy, but said she would call her. I felt good about being direct and telling Mom to speak for herself. THIS IS IMPROVEMENT.*

Be creative with this section. You will find that a great deal of healing and recovery can and will take place as you work in this section with the members of your family.

17
Influential Persons

The purpose of the influential persons section is to provide a place in the FIS for the ACoA to work out issues with people who are not family members. Even though the alcoholic family tries to remain isolated from society, it does not live in a vacuum, and other people often have a great impact on the lives of the family members. Influential persons may have had either a positive or a negative effect on the ACoA.

Many ACoAs have had people in their lives who have had strong positive effects on them. These influential persons are often schoolteachers who befriend the ACoA, clergy who tried to help, and neighbors who have been kind. Sometimes total strangers who have been kind and helpful to the ACoA have had a lasting positive influence. In this section the ACoA can remain in contact with these positive influences even though distance, death, or other reasons prevent it.

Clare, an ACoA, remembered a woman who lived across the street from her who would let her stay in her house when her mother and father were late coming home—which happened often. Clare remembered this woman's kindness and warmth and would often go to her house when her parents fought. To Clare this neighbor became a person with whom she felt safe, and she was very sad when her family moved to another town. Clare used this section to reestablish communication with this woman and to thank her for her kindness.

There are also influential persons who have had powerful negative impact on ACoAs. Because of the nature of the alcoholic family, the family often cannot protect its children from outsiders who wish to do the children harm. Children in alcoholic families are open and vulnerable to that segment of the population who prey upon children. These are those people who molest, rape, and physically or emotionally abuse children. If the child in an alcoholic family is hurt by an outsider, the family does not know how to help the child to resolve the emotional trauma. (See Chapter 7 on chronic shock for more details.) The ACoA can use this section to help in resolving this childhood emotional trauma.

By using the techniques of dialoguing and letter writing to allow repressed emotions to be released, the ACoA can let go of the anger, the hurt, and the rage that is often held inside. The letting go of those painful, stored-up emotions is a large part of the healing process. Both dialoguing and letter writing have been discussed in detail in earlier sections of this book. The techniques remain basically the same.

One difference, however, is in the dialoguing. Often the milestones of an influential person may not be known, and there is almost no possibility of finding out any information about the person. In cases such as this skip milestones and proceed directly to dialoguing. Where there is no information about an influential person, letter writing would be the method of choice to use for the resolution of unresolved issues. Be creative in the use of techniques. I encourage you to try out your ideas and adapt the methods explained and outlined in the FIS to your own situations.

18
Affirmations

We are what we think. There is a great deal of power in the thoughts, spoken words, and written statements that we make about ourselves. A direct correlation exists between the way a person thinks and how he or she behaves. It is difficult for many of us to imagine how much of our own reality we create by how we think and speak.

Current research does, however, indicate that to a large extent we create our own realities with our thoughts. Research in the health sciences definitely proves that thoughts and attitudes contribute to the healing process and that these same thoughts and attitudes can also contribute to ill health. The difference is whether these thoughts are positive or negative.

The alcoholic family is a hotbed of negative thinking and behavior. The children who are raised in this system learn, at a very early age, that they are worthless and that as individuals they are no good. To say that most ACoAs have a poor self-image is an understatement; at every front the alcoholic family batters its children with negative thinking. The negative thinking becomes so ingrained in ACoAs that it becomes unconscious. This unconscious programming stays with these children all of their lives. The unconscious programming can, however, be changed, and using affirmations is one of the most powerful ways to produce this change.

Affirmations are positive thoughts that a person deliberately introduces into his or her consciousness so that the old negative programming is replaced by new, positive programming.

ACoAs' negative programming runs deep and comes about directly as a result of being raised in an alcoholic family. As a child, the ACoA, like all children, received both verbal and nonverbal messages from the important adults in his or her life. Many times these messages were translated into negative programming. As adults this negative programming is still carried around in the unconscious mind.

Affirmations can, over a period of time, replace those old negative programs. It is vital to remember that affirmations are not used to repress feelings; they are not used to stuff emotions. ACoAs have a great deal of experience with how to stuff feelings and emotions—they don't need another technique. The process of releasing stuffed negative emotions must occur for the ACoA to grow. Affirmations create a new and fresh point of view rather than just replace the old ideas. Creating this new point of view is called cognitive reconstruction.

There are a number of different ways to do affirmations. Although the FIS is primarily set up for writing, I feel that all aspects, including writing affirmations, need to be learned by the ACoA. The ways to use affirmations that I have found the most effective are:

1. Spoken silently to oneself.
2. Said out loud.
3. Spoken out loud to another person.
4. Spoken into a recorder and played back.
5. Written down on paper.

The following statements are guidelines to using affirmations.

1. Affirmations are positive statements. We teach people to affirm the positive, rather than reinforce the negative.
2. Affirmations are most effective when they are short and to the point. Keep them simple.
3. Affirmations are kept in the present.

4. Affirmations affirm what one desires rather than what one wants to get rid of.
5. Affirmations take time to get results. They should not be put on a timetable; the results will unfold at their own speed.
6. Affirmations are repeated each day. It is the repetition of the positive affirmation that produces the desired result.

An ACoA named Helen was married to an alcoholic. Her husband had been sober for four years but had returned to drinking, and had been drinking for about two years when Helen came to me for counseling.

Like many ACoAs, Helen had an extremely low self-image. She could not imagine what she could do to change her current living situation, but she knew that she had to do something because she was lost in a lot of emotional pain. Like many women in her situation, she also blamed herself for her husband's drinking problem.

After Helen and I had been in two counseling sessions, we worked out a simple affirmation that she could do at home and at work. The affirmation was "I, Helen, love myself."

Helen's instructions were to say this affirmation ten times to herself every morning.

> *I, Helen, love myself.*
> *I, Helen, love myself.*
> *I, Helen, love myself.*
> *I, Helen, love myself.*
> *I, Helen, love myself.*
> *I, Helen, love myself.*
> *I, Helen, love myself.*
> *I, Helen, love myself.*
> *I, Helen, love myself.*
> *I, Helen, love myself.*

Helen's self-image was so poor that at first she was unable to say the affirmation out loud. After a number of weeks she could say the affirmation out loud to herself, at which point I had her say the affirmation aloud each morning while looking into her bedroom mirror.

It was a major turning point in Helen's life when, during a counseling session, she was able to look at me in the eye and tell me, "I, Helen, love myself."

Each ACoA is different, and affirmations should be tailored to individual needs. In Helen's case we needed to start very gently, with her saying the affirmation first silently to herself, then out loud to the mirror, and finally out loud to me.

Over the months that Helen and I were in the counseling relationship, she continued to do her affirmation and her feelings of self-love got stronger and stronger. The result of this work was that Helen finally left the unhealthy relationship and rebuilt her life. I received a telephone call from her a year after she moved out of town and she was doing fine—and still is doing her affirmation.

The affirmation "I love myself" is an important one for ACoAs. Most ACoAs have very little regard for themselves, and this love affirmation is very helpful in changing the old programming. This affirmation is also very powerful when written ten times each day.

I have gotten some very positive feedback from ACoAs who have used their affirmations in creative ways. A powerful method for using affirmations is to have the ACoA record the affirmation onto a tape and play the tape back at convenient times, such as while driving to and from work or when doing housework. As the tape is being played you can either listen or say the affirmation along with the recording.

The most powerful way to use an affirmation is to write it down on paper. This method strongly reinforces the affirmation because as it is being written, it is seen, said to one's self, and felt as the act of writing is taking place. This is the section of the FIS where affirmations are written.

Changes in attitude and point of view occur very rapidly with ACoAs who use written affirmations. Written affirmations are most effective when written ten to twenty times each day. I am partial to morning, but anytime during the day is effective. (I choose morning because if I don't do things then, I have a tendency never to get around to them.)

Do not become overloaded with affirmations. Doing four or five affirmations at one time can be very time-consuming and discouraging. Working on one or two affirmations at a time is best.

To be most powerful the written affirmation is done in the first person (I), the second person (you), and the third person (he or she). Here is an example involving an ACoA named Steven. Like many ACoAs, Steven was having a difficult time getting in touch with his emotions. He felt very stuck. He knew that he was blocking emotions, but he did not know how to get unstuck.

The affirmation that we worked out for Steven was:

I, Steven, am capable and willing to experience all of my emotions.

This part of the affirmation is written in the first person and makes the statement that even with old negative ideas about being unable to express emotions, he, Steven, is affirming that today he can express emotions. (Remember that to be effective, affirmations are done in the present tense.)

You, Steven, are capable and willing to experience all of your emotions.

This part of the affirmation is written in the second person and makes the statement that, although Steven was once taught that showing emotions was unacceptable be-havior, today he is allowed to show emotions.

He, Steven, is capable and willing to express all of his emotions.

This part of the affirmation is written in the third person and makes the statement that regardless of the role mod-els that Steven had and regardless of what people said about him, Steven is capable and willing to express his emotions today.

The whole affirmation would be:

> *I, Steven, am capable and willing to experience all of my emotions.*
>
> *You, Steven, are capable and willing to experience all of your emotions.*
>
> *He, Steven, is capable and willing to express all of his emotions.*

An important point to remember is that when strong, positive affirmations are used, they will in most cases bring up strong, negative feelings from the person's subconscious. When people who have had strong negative programming, such as ACoAs, use positive affirmations, the negative feelings that are a part of that old programming will surface. This is particularly true when the affirmation is being written.

When writing an affirmation, it is important to acknowledge these negative feelings. This acknowledgment is an integrated part of the process of letting go of the old programming. I have found that jotting down the negative thoughts after writing the affirmation is the most effective method of noting the negative response.

After the affirmation has been written, along with the negative responses, the negative responses can be reviewed. This will give insights into the unconscious negative programming that is standing in the way of the fulfillment of the affirmation. After the negative responses have been written for approximately four days, you will have a good idea of what is standing in the way of the affirmation. At this point discontinue writing the negative responses and just write the affirmation.

The negative responses that surface during writing the affirmations make excellent material for discussion during counseling sessions and at ACoAs groups.

Often, as the affirmation is being written, the negative responses will transform into more positive responses. During this process of moving from the negative to the positive, the ACoA may even find that he or she is writing encouraging statements about the affirmation.

Continuing to use Steven as an example, the affirmation and his responses were as follows:

> *I, Steven, am capable and willing to experience all of my emotions.* (No, I can't do that.)
> *You, Steven, are capable and willing to experience all of your emotions.* (I was told that it was bad to show emotions.)
> *He, Steven, is capable and willing to express all of his emotions.* (No I'm not.)

> *I, Steven, am capable and willing to experience all of my emotions.* (What if someone sees me cry?)
> *You, Steven, are capable and willing to experience all of your emotions.* (I'm afraid to let people in.)
> *He, Steven, is capable and willing to express all of his emotions.* (I feel so sad.)

> *I, Steven, am capable and willing to experience all of my emotions.* (Dad never cried.)
> *You, Steven, are capable and willing to experience all of your emotions.* (This makes me feel sick.)
> *He, Steven, is capable and willing to express all of1 his emotions.* (I won't be a man if I feel.)

> *I, Steven, am capable and willing to experience all of my emotions.* (I'm afraid of what's bottled up inside of me.)
> *You, Steven, are capable and willing to experience all of your emotions.* (I'll lose control.)
> *He, Steven, is capable and willing to express all of his emotions.* (The last time I cried, I was ten.)

> *I, Steven, am capable and willing to experience all of my emotions.* (Maybe I can.)
> *You, Steven, are capable and willing to experience all of your emotions.* (It might not be so bad.)
> *He, Steven, is capable and willing to express all of his emotions.* (I think I will be able to.)

As can be seen in the above example, while Steven was writing his affirmation, he moved from the negative responses that he wrote in the beginning to more positive and encouraging responses.

Change can happen quickly when affirmations are used. Not only can affirmations be used to root out the old negative programming that ACoAs have, but they can also be used to deal with immediate situations that cause fearful responses.

One ACoA, Kim, called me on the phone and told me that she wanted to call a man that she was interested in to ask him to a party, but she was afraid to make the call. She had to make the call that night because the party was the next day. I asked her what kind of affirmation would fit this situation, and she created this affirmation:

> *I, Kim, can ask Joe for a date.*

She wrote this several times, and then made the telephone call.

Most ACoAs have difficulties in relationships. Some excellent affirmations to use with difficult relationships are:

> *I _____, am a healthy person, and I am capable of having a loving, intimate relationship.*
> *I, _____, no longer need _____ to make me feel good about myself.*
> *I love myself and I deserve a good relationship.*

Affirmations are not really very new. People have been using them for years, even in the addictions field. How many times have you heard "I, _____, am clean and sober today"? Now, that's a powerful affirmation.

Most ACoAs really enjoy doing affirmations. It gives them an extremely positive payoff for doing a small amount of work and helps them feel good about themselves. Affirmations give the ACoA an opportunity to take a visible, active part in their recovery process.

The following is a list of some of the affirmations that are useful for ACoAs.

Every day in every way I am getting better, better, and better.

I can accept all of my feelings as part of myself.

The more I love myself, the more I am capable of loving.

I am a whole, healthy human being.

My life is unfolding as it should.

I, _____, am lovable.

I, _____, am loving.

I, _____, deserve love.

My true self is my sober self.

My life has meaning and purpose.

I am living my life one day at a time.

Today I can stay sober and happy.

I have a right to be here in the world.

I am the right sex.

Be creative and add your own affirmations to the above list.

Many ACoAs have a spiritual unrest within them, and almost to a person, they have a desire to grow in a spiritual direction. Affirmations used in a spiritual context are powerful. I have found that ACoAs who seek to expand and grow spiritually use this type of affirmation with great enthusiasm and effectiveness. Below are some examples of affirmations that have a spiritual dimension and direction.

My higher self is guiding me in everything I do.

The Christ within me is creating miracles in my life today.

I am letting go and letting God.

I , _____, am living in the presence of divine love and light.

I, _____, am at one with the spirit of the universe.

The affirmations section of the FIS can be very powerful. In this section the ACoA can begin, and to a great extent complete, the process of replacing the negative programming learned in the alcoholic family with a more positive way of looking at the world. This is an important component of treatment for the adult children of alcoholics syndrome.

Remember, be creative with this section. Create your own affirmations; create ones that fit your needs and wishes. No one really knows what limits there are in using affirmations. If used correctly, your recovery will be both faster and more joyful.

19
Spiritual Reflections

In this section of the FIS, the ACoA has the opportunity to reflect upon the relationship that he or she has with a Higher Power, or God. Many ACoAs have difficulty with coming to terms with a Higher Power. When they look at their past experiences and reexperience some of the pain of their childhood, it is often difficult for them to recognize and accept that a loving and caring Higher Power operates in the universe. Many ACoAs are either angry at God or refuse to think about the existence of a Higher Power. They ask questions like "Why did God do this to me?" or "How could God do this to an innocent child?"

Acknowledging anger and rage at God is often the first step in developing a philosophy that is encompassing enough to allow for the existence of all things and all occurrences. Being aware and acknowledging the anger, however, is just the first step, and is often not enough. The anger and rage must be shared and expressed for release to occur. Sharing these feelings of anger with other ACoAs and with sympathetic religious leaders is often the key to letting go of the anger and rage that ACoAs feel toward God. Trying to think through the anger and be rational about it often does nothing but repress it, and then the anger and rage will just reappear at some future point.

A powerful technique for expressing this anger and rage is writing a letter to God and telling Him exactly why the anger is there. This is one of the major uses of this section of the FIS. Of course, the letter is not mailed—I haven't found an earthly address yet—and is kept in this section for future reflection. Most ACoAs feel very hesitant about expressing anger at God. It must be remembered, however, that with the expression of anger and rage, the release of that anger and rage often happens. It is with this release that new realms of the spirit open for the ACoA.

Dialoguing with the Higher Power is another technique for opening up communications with a spiritual force. This technique has been used by many ACoAs to reestablish a spiritual communication. Both letter writing and dialoguing have been explained in previous sections, and will not be reexplained at this point. There is, however, one variation in dialoguing with your Higher Power or whatever name you choose to call the Spiritual Force. Most ACoAs find it more comfortable to leave out the creating of milestones. For many, including myself, creating milestones for the Supreme Creator of the universe is rather presumptuous. With this exception the instructions for letter writing and dialoguing still stand.

In this section I have decided not to include examples of letters and dialogues written by ACoAs. I have done this because I feel that each ACoA has the right to explore his or her own concept of God without being influenced by either myself or others. I am confident that ACoAs will find and come to some kind of peace with their spiritual aspect. I have seen this happen again and again with ACoAs, and this spiritual awareness is an integrated part of recovery.

The basic conflict that many ACoAs feel is, If God is loving and all-powerful, then how could I have been put through so much pain as a child? This conflict is a spiritual paradox, and it is almost impossible to find an answer to this question from an external source. The answer must come from within. And the answer will come. It has been my experience—both personally and in sharing the experiences of the ACoAs whom I have worked with over the years—that through active reflection the spiritual *dis-ease* of ACoAs is often where this resolution begins.

20
Integration

In this, the last section of the FIS, the writer has a place where he or she can write about what has happened as a result of working through his or her ACoAs issues. This section is where renewal and integration are recorded. Here the ACoA writes about not only the issues dealt with in the FIS, but also what is being worked on in therapy, and during ACoAs groups. Integration is the healing process, and here is where the ACoA records how this healing process is happening in his or her life.

It is important for the ACoA to record progress—to record the triumphs and insights that are a testament to the recovery process. When unhealthy patterns in relationships are recognized and released, here is where that realization is recorded. When forgiveness replaces anger and hurt, here is where that transformation is recorded. When an ACoA demands direct communication from a family who previously communicated by silence and innuendo, here is where that triumph is recorded. Here, in the integration section, is where the ACoA records the progress and the "Ah-ha" experience that releases him or her from the chains that bind him or her to the past.

It is in the integration section that the ACoA can record the emotional realization, which generally happens long after the intellectual realization, that alcoholism is a disease, and that he or she was powerless over what happened as a child. Here the ACoA can come to terms with old ideas about God, and form a relationship with God that can be fruitful and loving.

The integration section is an open-ended section. Like the rest of the system, this section can be used whenever the ACoA wishes. There is no real structure to this section, and the writer is encouraged to allow this section to develop and grow without structure. The only structure I have found useful in this section is to date each integration entry. I also know of some ACoAs who do not even date these entries. It is up to you, the writer, to develop this section in whatever way you see fit. Most of the other sections in the FIS are structured, and the structure is important. Without it many ACoAs would not be able to use a writing system effectively. In this section, however, structure is cast away so the ACoA can freely record the unfolding of a healthier way of life.

The following are some integration entries that have been made by ACoAs.

It feels so good to stand up to my family and say that I am an adult, and that I demand that I be treated as an adult. It feels so good at last to do this.

I now have a real relationship with my sister. We really talk about how we feel about things now, rather than just talking around in circles.

I really forgive my father. What he did to me was wrong, I know that I was blameless, and I now have let go of the anger and the fear. I'm not sure that I love him, but I do forgive him.

I can now talk to my wife and kids about how I feel and what is going on with us as a family. I never could do that before, either in this, my present family, or in my family of origin.

There is a movement, a motion in my life, that is coming to completion. It is putting away the old ways of living and stepping out into the world with the confidence and experience of having lived and learned. This confidence stems from much more than just the past experiences of my life. It is knowing that the

*events of my life and I are one with each other, and
that through this I have learned to love myself. Now
it is time for me to love the universe. Just as it was
necessary to love those things about me that I per-
ceived as imperfect, I now am learning to love all of
the world, even those parts that I see as imperfect.
There are no imperfect parts of me or of the world. All
there are are different parts in different stages of development. Everything is right on time, right on schedule.
Being free and joyful in this continuing process of unfolding is most important. The issues that are at hand in
myself and the world are very important—too important
to take seriously. A sense of humor is a must. I will laugh
deeply and loudly, I will share and love. I am free.*

21
Conclusion

Recovery from the adult children of alcoholics syndrome is a process. It is a gradual awakening rather than an event. Although recovery is often filled with moments of sharp, clear insights, and sometimes blazing realizations, for the most part, and for most ACoAs, recovery is learning to live life from a new and different point of view, one day at a time.

Being raised in an alcoholic family is often a devastating experience. Those who have survived this experience are people who do not lack in either creativity or courage. They truly are survivors. The challenge for these people, the survivors, is to use the skills and techniques that they developed in new and more creative ways of living. Their challenge is to be open, to learn new skills, and to experiment with different points of view.

The letting go of the pain and fear is a necessary part of the recovery process for the ACoA. As the pain and fear are released happiness, freedom, and joy become a way of life, rather than just words spoken or read. I have seen this happen again and again with ACoAs who have worked at their recovery. And work is needed. Recovery does not happen by just thinking about it or wanting it. Recovery occurs through working and by being available to experience pain. It is painful to grow through ACoA issues, but this pain—the pain of growth—is clean and it is healing. At the other side of the pain of growth is joy and the love of life. This is the reward for walking through the pain of growth.

Ultimately the decision to work through ACoA issues is an act of faith and a spiritual commitment. For the ACoA this decision means risking going into territory that has not been explored. This is the territory of the unconscious, the territory of new and different ways of being and living—it is the territory of inner self. This territory of inner self must be experienced to be known. With the experience of knowing one's inner self comes a sense of love and joy that must be experienced to be understood.

Just as a map is not the territory but a guide to the territory, I hope this book will prove to be a map to the territory of self for Adult Children of Alcoholics.

Wayne Kritsberg
February 1986

Resources

Every day more and more resources become available for adult children of alcoholics. For this reason, it is almost impossible to keep an up-to-date resource list. Below are three established organizations that have information about ACoAs activities on national and local levels. These organizations will generally be able to assist ACoAs in contacting local ACoAs groups. Local Councils on Alcoholism and Drug Abuse, local addictions treatment programs, Alcoholics Anonymous, and Al-Anon groups will frequently be able to provide local-level information on ACoAs activities. Check the telephone book for these telephone numbers.

Al-Anon Family Group Headquarters
P.O. Box 862
Midtown Station
New York, New York 10018–0862

RESOURCES

Local resources for Adult Children of Alcoholics can be found by looking in the telephone book, by inquiring at Al-Anon or Alcoholics Anonymous meetings, or by contracting a local addictions treatment program.

TO THE READER

It is not always possible for me to answer the mail I receive from readers. However, I greatly appreciate learning about your experiences in working with this material. If you would like to share your experience, please write to: Wayne Kritsberg, 10121 Whitecap Dr. NW, Olympia, WA 98502.

ABOUT THE AUTHOR

WAYNE KRITSBERG, M.A. is a therapist, author, and lecturer. He is internationally recognized for his innovative work with adult children of alcoholics and adult survivors of childhood sexual trauma. Wayne is a consultant to chemical dependency and trauma treatment programs. He leads counselor training and personal recovery workshops throughout the international community.

Wayne is author of the books *Healing Together: A Guide to Intimacy and Recovery for Co-Dependent Couples, Gifts for Personal Growth and Recovery, Gifts: Advanced Skills for Alcoholism Counselors;* and the popular booklets *Chronic Shock and Adult Children of Alcoholics* and *Am I in a Co-Dependent Relationship?* He is also author of *The Invisible Wound: A New Approach to Healing Childhood Sexual Trauma* and is co-author of *A Quiet Strength,* a men's meditational.

Wayne's experience includes directing a hospital emergency room counseling center, managing a halfway house for alcoholics and addicts, and clinical consulting. He maintains an active private practice where he focuses on healing childhood trauma. Wayne lives with his family in the Olympia, Washington area.

BANTAM BOOKS ON
ADDICTION AND RECOVERY

Please ask your bookseller for the books you have missed.

ADDICTION

The most up-to-date information from the leading experts in the field.

UNDER THE INFLUENCE
A Guide to the Myths and Realities of Alcoholism
James R. Milam, Ph.D., and Katherine Ketcham
This groundbreaking classic emphasizes treating alcoholism as a physiological disease and offers information on how to tell if someone is an alcoholic, treatment, and recovery.
27487-2   *Paperback* $7.99/$11.99 in Canada

ADULT CHILDREN

Essential reading for the millions who grew up in dysfunctional families.

THE ADULT CHILDREN OF ALCOHOLICS SYNDROME
Wayne Kritsberg
Real help and hope for adult children in a complete self-help program that shows how to recognize and remedy the effects of the dysfunctional family.
27279-9   *Paperback* $7.50/$10.99 in Canada

FAMILY ISSUES

Groundbreaking books on conquering co-dependence and helping addicted family members.

TOXIC PARENTS
Overcoming Their Hurtful Legacy and Reclaiming Your Life
Dr. Susan Forward with Craig Buck
The challenging, compassionate, and controversial new guide to recognizing and recovering from the lasting damage caused by physical or emotional abuse in childhood, by bestselling author of *Men Who Hate Women & the Women Who Love Them*.
38140-7   *Paperback* $13.95/$21.00 in Canada

HEALING RELATIONSHIP

Books that point readers toward a healthier self and new ways of relating with others.

HOW TO BREAK YOUR ADDICTION TO A PERSON
Howard M. Halpern, Ph.D.
An insightful, step-by-step guide to breaking painful addictive relationships—and surviving separation.
26005-7   *Paperback* $7.50/$10.99 in Canada

OUT OF DARKNESS INTO THE LIGHT
A Journey of Inner Healing
Gerald G. Jampolsky, M.D.
The bestselling author of *Love is Letting Go of Fear* offers a blue-print for recovery through his personal journey from severe depression, guilt, and alcohol abuse to a triumphant rediscovery of self and inner healing.
34791-8   *Paperback* $19.00/$28.00 in Canada

BECOMING NATURALLY THERAPEUTIC
A Return to the True Essence of Helping
Jacquelyn Small
The renown workshop leader's inspiring guide for all who serve as listeners or counselors in the lives of others. Basing her work on landmark studies, Small helps us "straight-talk" beyond our co-dependent or controlling ways of helping others and teaches how to offer clear and loving guidance directly from the heart.
34800-0   *Paperback* $15.95/$23.95 in Canada

<u>MEDITATIONALS</u>

Daily inspiration and guidance based on the 12-step programs.

A NEW DAY
365 Meditations for Personal and Spiritual Growth
Anonymous
Offers spiritual and psychological guidance on overcoming the struggles we face each day, by the author of *A Day at a Time*.
34591-5   *Paperback* $10.95/$16.95 in Canada

Prices subject to change.